SYSTEMS THEORY, SCIENCE, AND SOCIAL WORK

by

IRMA STEIN, D.S.W.

With a Foreword by
Herbert S. Strean

The Scarecrow Press, Inc.
Metuchen, N. J.   1974

Library of Congress Cataloging in Publication Data

Stein, Irma L
  Systems theory, science, and social work.

  Includes bibliographical references.
  1. Social service. 2. System analysis.
3. Psychiatry. I. Title.
HV41.S782   361'.001   73-15581
ISBN 0-8108-0660-6

CONTENTS

iii

iv

FOREWORD

As any practitioner or scholar in social work and its allied fields knows, the modal units of diagnostic and therapeutic attention have shown dramatic changes in the last two decades. From an almost exclusive preoccupation with the client or patient's internal dynamics, workers have begun to appreciate the saliency of interpersonal dyads and larger units such as the family, as they affect and are affected by the client's psychosocial functioning.

Inevitably, the utility of systems theory to social workers and others became apparent by the late 1950's. Particularly could those interested in family functioning, interaction in small groups, and community life recognize how concepts from systems theory like homeostasis, stability, transaction, and communication of information, could be applied to the study, diagnosis, and treatment of their clients and client systems.

Social workers have always alleged that their unique expertise was understanding and relating to the person-in-his-situation. Systems theory has provided an extremely helpful framework for the worker as he attempts to understand how situational variables affect the person and vice versa. More than any other social science contribution, systems theory has exposed how individuals' adaptive and maladaptive functioning is influenced by the setting he is in.

One of the pioneers and leaders in the applicability of systems theory to social work has been Dr. Irma Stein.

Her monumental three-volume study on the agency as a social system was one of the first clear expositions on how social workers and clients participate in transactions which are influenced by many sub-systems variables, that were hardly considered before her study was undertaken. In addition to demonstrating the formal and informal transactions among workers and clients in a social agency, Professor Stein was the first to demonstrate the system properties of the psychiatric consultation process in social agencies and clinics.

Over the years Professor Stein has contributed much understanding on how many psychological and social problems that confront workers in the human service professions can be more profoundly diagnosed with the use of systems theory. She has also demonstrated how systems theory provides targets for entry and goals for worker and client.

In this text, we have a clear distillation of Professor Stein's years of research, practice and teaching in the use of systems theory. This book not only provides a comprehensive review of the major concepts of systems theory but shows its strengths and limitations, its relationship to other social science orientations, and when it can stand alone. This text, I am sure, will not only be of much assistance to the scholar of human functioning and interaction but to the student and practitioner who wants to learn more about how to understand and relate to the person-in-his-situation.

Herbert S. Strean, D. S. W.
Graduate School of Social Work
Rutgers University
New Brunswick, New Jersey

INTRODUCTION

This book was initially conceived as a concise chapter on systems theory and social work. The fact that it went further, that the chapter emerged into a book, was not "consciously planned." In retrospect it would seem that a number of factors, operating together, contributed to this metamorphosis. It may be useful to pinpoint some of these--thereby anticipating questions and/or concerns of the reader.

Although the beginning section on systems theory incorporates and defines basic concepts and principles, the latter are presented from the perspective of the writer's focus on systems theory trends and related scientific and professional issues. In other words, the book is primarily concerned with developments in systems theory, which are explicated and extended in the analyses of professional applications of systems theory and in the presentations of various innovations and modifications of theoretical constructs. In essence then, the conception is that of "a systems view of the world"[1] over time. This perspective demanded a more comprehensive and exacting exposition than could be encompassed within the confines of a single chapter. Moreover, it led to a new level of analysis which, in turn, enlarged the scope of the manuscript.

Such an orientation and approach may pose some difficulties for the reader unfamiliar with systems theory and its terminology. Hopefully, this type of difficulty will be solved by the explanations and illustrations, elaborations and comparative analyses, and as selected themes are delineated, reiterated, and interwoven throughout the entire book.

Another type of difficulty may also be anticipated. The analysis of issues and dilemmas, as these are reflected in professional disciplines such as social work and psychiatry, highlights inconsistencies and discrepancies in conceptual notions and practice applications. Stated differently, particular attention is given to confusions and/or distortions involving scientific theory, professional ideology and values, and interventive patterns and behaviors. The processes of testing and assessment may require the reader to re-examine familiar and accepted ideas and commitments. The author believes that theoretical and "action" notions must be made explicit, in order that positions may be responsibly undertaken. It is also essential, however, to remain open to new and/or revised input, i.e., to abstract, middle range, or empirical levels of data-information. This problem of simultaneously maintaining scientific rigor and operational flexibility suggests that compromises and syntheses occur frequently as a "functional necessity."

It is important to keep in mind that it is not always possible or even desirable to be totally consistent, nor, on the other hand, to strive for a "harmonizing synthesis" of antagonistic values. Kolakowski[2] states that "it is only thanks to inconsistency that humanity has kept alive on this earth" (pp. 206, 202). His comments are especially pertinent in introducing the reader to a book such as this which stresses the significance of inconsistencies in the analyses of scientific theories, operational concepts, practice applications, and their relationship to normative values.

Inconsistency is simply a hidden awareness of the contradictions of this world.... In so far as inconsistency is an individual attitude, it is nothing but a collection of uncertainties which conscience keeps in reserve, a continuous awareness that one may be mistaken or that the enemy may be right. We have in mind here the relations between thought and principle on the one hand and practical behavior on the other ... there exist values that are mutually exclusive without ceasing to be values, whereas truths cannot be mutually exclusive without ceasing to be truths [p. 204].

Finally, in his considerations of conflicting loyalties, Kolakowski points out that "apparent and deceiving syntheses are embraced so that we may seem consistent with ourselves" (p. 208). It would appear, thus, that we must continue to search for truths, to be consciously aware of the nature of our inconsistencies while accepting the fact that "contradictions [will] haunt us as long as we act within a world of values, or simply as long as we exist" (p. 206).

Notes

1. Since the completion of this manuscript, The Systems View of the World by Ervin Laszlo, published in 1972, was made available to the writer. As a scientist and philosopher, Laszlo offers an exposition that is quite consistent with the systems theory-model presented in this book. That is, the basic concepts, laws, and propositions are very similar to those of systems theorists cited in the following pages, e.g., Bertalanffy, Miller, Rapoport, Ashby, et al. While terminology (e.g., classification of types of systems) differs, the meanings are almost identical. Laszlo, thus, provides still another "view" of systems theory which includes such notions as system levels, system hierarchy, "invariances" and isomorphisms, and which is concerned with the continuities and discontinuities of man and nature within an ecological and evolutionary frame of reference.

2. "In Praise of Inconsistency," Leszek Kolakowski, Dissent, Spring 1964, pp. 201-209.

PART I

SYSTEMS THEORY AND THE SYSTEMS MODEL

In 1972 the literature devoted to general systems
theory (typically used interchangeably with systems theory)
which explicates its nature, principles, laws, and concepts,
as well as its diverse applications (proposed and "tested")
in various scientific fields and professional disciplines is
voluminous, if not overwhelming. There are ample systems writings for the researcher and practitioner in "first-
hand" scientific, scholarly sources and also in numerous
journals and periodicals of a wide range of applied fields,
such as engineering, psychiatry, and social work.[1] The
writer has drawn from materials of both types and as a
consequence has been intrigued by the many different, sometimes overlapping, compatible, and inconsistent notions that
prevail. The primary aim of this book is to present certain trends and some selected issues that deserve the consideration of social workers today. The intent is not to
offer the reader a complete, systematic exposition of systems theory nor a comprehensive critique of its applications.
However, the delineation of systems theory in terms of the
questions and dilemmas, along with the answers and solutions it has suggested, have import for the current state
and direction of social work theory and practice.

1

It is this conviction that directed the selection of material that follows. After brief initial comments on the notions of system, the discussion will focus on general systems theory, its origins and development. Thus, matters of scientific theory, models, methods, and values come into play, especially as they are reflected in the position and terminology[2] of the scientific-observer-intervener. In the following section, applications and utilizations of systems theory will be given attention. Here, too, the purpose is to factor out the common patterns and different emphases. The next part of the book extends the discussion of systems theory from a broader perspective. It considers the "changing faces" of theory--old and new, concepts and semantics; selected trends, issues and their implications reappear here in a different light and in a different context. The book will close with a brief concluding statement.

Chapter 1

DEVELOPMENTS IN SYSTEMS THEORY

THE CONCEPT OF SYSTEM

The concept of system has received wide acceptance in scientific and professional disciplines. System is typically understood as a whole made up of interdependent and interacting parts. Thus, it is more than an aggregate of elements since the whole is greater than the sum of its parts. Depending upon the nature of the relationships among the parts, the whole has particular "emergent" characteristics or qualities by which it is generally recognizable and identifiable.

There are innumerable definitions of the concept of system. The classic definition of von Bertalanffy presented in 1956 (11, p. 2) is: "a set of units with relationships among them." Miller notes that the "word set implies that the units have common properties. The state of each unit is constrained by, conditioned by, or dependent on the state of other units" (58, p. 200). Despite the similarities of many definitions, the differences in emphases should be noted. A system may be viewed basically in structural terms as a set of interrelated elements, or it may be viewed in terms of its performance, particularly input-output activities (35, p. 370). While Gross believes that these two approaches can be brought together in the definition of a system as a set of interrelated elements with a capacity for

3

certain kinds of performance, it will be seen that these
two emphases may represent incompatible views of reality
and therefore lead to different orientations to professional
practice.   It might also be noted here that questions have
been raised about the degree of wholeness--to what extent
the "degree of entitivity" is related to the nature of the
relationships of the parts of the system to each other and
the parts to the system as a whole, as well as to what
extent this degree of wholeness is related to system level
("simple or complex") (19, pp. 42-45).[3]

A final illustration will demonstrate different ways
that the definition of system has been interpreted and
utilized.   Rabkin, a social psychiatrist, states that because

> ... epigenetics[4] concerns itself with systems ...
> that are performances rather than objects or
> structures, any discussion of development or char-
> acteristics of a single entity cannot be epigenetic
> since by definition a system or organization con-
> sists of two things standing in relationship to
> each other [69, p. 106].

Thus Rabkin understands "two things" only at the level of
social systems, whereas system as a whole consisting of
interdependent and interacting parts, or as a set of units
with relationships among them, may refer to the organism
or personality system level.   Stated differently, the fact
that living systems maintain constant interchange with other
systems in their environment does not negate the notion of
epigenetics as applied to the development of a "single
entity."   Thus it would seem that notions of system, the
environment, and the change process are determined, at
least to some extent, by the professional discipline and
conceptual orientation of the author-observer.

Concepts of space and time, matter-energy, and information underpin the concept of system. Living systems (one type of concrete or empirical system)[5] are made up of matter and energy organized by information, and they exist in space and time. They have boundaries which are at least partially permeable, thus permitting transmissions of matter energy or information to cross them (see 58).[6]

Although it may seem that these conceptual phenomena are noncontroversial, scrutiny of the literature indicates that they often are at the heart of disagreements within and between the scientific and professional disciplines. It may be concluded therefore that concepts of space, time, matter-energy, and information determine and are determined by one's theory-model of reality and notions of causality and change. For example, abstracted systems are common in the social sciences, which are oriented toward relationships, whereas the natural sciences (e.g., physiology, biology) are conceived as concrete systems which emphasize spatial arrangements and structure. Miller observes that:

> ... functionalists may resist the use of space-time coordinates because they seem static. But one must have such coordinates in order to observe and measure process. Subjectivists may resist such coordinates because their private experience does not seem to be presented to them in external space-time. But where else do their inputs arise? [58, p. 76].

As suggested above, all systems are characterized by structure and process. As will be seen, these concepts also have been the basis for much disagreement, some of which is associated with different notions of general systems theory and some of which appears to be a matter of semantic differences arising out of the particular perspective of the theoretician-practitioner.   Structure has been defined as:

> ... the arrangement of a system's subsystems and
> components in three-dimensional space at a given
> moment in time. Process is all change over time
> of matter-energy or information in a system. Pro-
> cess may be viewed as encompassing both function
> and history; function being the reversible actions
> succeeding from moment to moment while history
> is the less readily reversed change such as growth,
> aging, and death. There is no one-to-one relation-
> ship between process and structure. But structure
> changes momentarily with functioning; when the
> change is irreversible there has been an historical
> process giving rise to a new structure [58, pp.
> 209, 218-19].

Thus, structure, function, and history, although differently
defined and utilized, are closely connected if not inseparable.
Gerard uses the terms being, behaving, and becoming in
place of the terms structure, function, and history. [7]
Grinker has summarized notions basic to the concept of
systems:

> A system is considered to be some whole form in
> structure or operation, concepts, or functions,
> composed of united and integrated parts. As such,
> it has an extent in time and space, and boundaries.
> A system has a past which is partly represented
> by its parts, for it develops or assembles from
> something preceding. It has a present, which is
> its existence as a relatively stable or what might
> be called resting form, and it has a future, that
> is its functional potentiality. In space form, struc-
> ture and dimensions constitute a framework which
> is relatively stable and timeless, yet only rela-
> tively so, for its constituents change during time
> but considerably slower than the novel or more
> active functions of the systems. To view the
> change of these functions through time, the frame
> or background may be artificially considered as
> stable [32, p. 370].

Finally, any discussion of the concepts of system must

include the important subject of the system-environment
relationship. The literature is replete with references to
the inseparability of the system and its environment. Thus,
any division between them is interpreted as conceptual and
arbitrary, depending upon the position-stance of the observer
and/or intervener. Grinker states that "a system is the
whole complex of the organism and environment ... both the
organism and environment are two parts of one system"
(32, p. 37). Hall and Fagen comment upon the question of

> ... when an object belongs to a system and when
> it belongs to the environment.... In a sense, a
> system together with its environment makes up the
> universe of all things of interest in a given context
> .... Any given system can be further subdivided
> into subsystems. Objects belonging to one system
> may well be considered as part of the environ-
> ment of another subsystem [37, pp. 83, 84].

The system-environment relationship has many ramifications;
for example, the issue of system levels[8] or hierarchy of
systems is a significant consideration in general systems
theory, in the applications of general systems theory, as
well as in current developments in the behavioral sciences
and professional disciplines.

GENERAL SYSTEMS THEORY

The scientific endeavors of von Bertalanffy, beginning
in the 1920's, culminated in his proposal of general systems
theory in 1956. He described it as "the formulation and
derivation of those principles which are valid for 'systems'
in general" (10, p. 130). The underlying notion here is that
"in certain aspects, corresponding abstractions and conceptual models can be applied to different phenomena. It is
only in view of these aspects that system laws will apply"

(11, p. 2). In 1962 he stated that "general systems theory
was conceived as a working hypothesis ... [as a] theoretical
model general systems theory has as its main function the
explanation, prediction and control of hitherto unexplored
phenomena" (12, p. 17).

Boulding also wrote on general systems theory in
1956 and pointed out that there had been an increasing need
for a body of systematic theoretical constructs which would

> ... discuss the general relationships of the empir-
> ical world.... It does not seek, of course, to
> establish a single, self-contained 'general theory
> of practically everything' which will replace all
> the special theories of particular disciplines....
> Since the optimum degree of generality in theory
> is not always reached by the particular sciences,
> general systems theory ... aims to point out simi-
> larities in the theoretical constructions of different
> disciplines, where these exist, and to develop
> theoretical models having applicability to at least
> two different fields of study.

General systems theory was conceived as a theory of interdisciplinary scope but it also "hopes to develop something
like a 'spectrum' of theories--a system of systems" (17,
p. 3).

In addition to the focus on the aims of general
systems theory as a theoretical model and a generalized
theory which interconnects the systems sciences and the
disciplinary sciences, thus enriching and enlarging these
sciences, it may also be defined and conceived as a method
of study. Reference to the systems methods of study was
implicit in the earlier statements regarding the search for
common patterns and similarities among systems. Rapoport
states that systems are studied from the three perspectives
of its structure, function, and evolution (70, p. xx). Grinker

defines three basic principles that may be applied to all
systems: the principle of stability, designated as homeostasis; the transactional principle, meaning all the recipro-
cating relationships reverberating in the system; and the
principle of communication of information (varying from signals characteristic of biological systems to symbols characteristic of social systems) (32, p. 372).

Boulding, also in 1956, writes of two approaches to
the organization of general systems theory, which he views
as complementary. The first approach is to look over the
empirical universe and to pick out certain general phenomena
which are found in many different disciplines, and to seek
to build up general theoretical models relevant to these
phenomena. "The second approach is to arrange the empirical fields in a hierarchy of complexity of organization
of their basic 'individual' or unit of behavior, and to try to
develop a level of abstraction appropriate to each" (17, p. 5).
Boulding illustrates these approaches: the first might ex-
plore the phenomenon of growth or the relationship between
the system and its suprasystem, or some other phenomenon
of almost universal significance for all disciplines; the
second is more systematic and it seeks to order systems
according to their hierarchy of complexity, in this way
finally leading to a system of systems (17, pp. 5-9).

Bertalanffy (in 1962) similarly discusses two methods
of general systems research. His empirico-intuitive method
has the advantage of remaining close to reality and thereby
can be easily illustrated and verified by examples from different fields of science. A second method in systems study
is utilized by Ashby. The latter follows a deductive method
which, instead of studying each empirical system with re-

spect to its universal principles, "considers the set of all
conceivable systems and then reduces the set to a more
reasonable size" (Ashby as quoted by Bertalanffy, 12, p. 15).
As might be expected, Bertalanffy notes the limitations of
this methodological approach rather than its advantages.
Essentially, he objects to Ashby's "machine theory" of life
as reflected in his systems approach. Further discussion
of this point relates to an analysis of general systems theory,
its origins and development as well as parallel theoretical
developments.

Precursors

There are two basic precursors to general systems
theory as it was evolved by Bertalanffy. The first was the
organismic viewpoint. While he wrote about organismic
biology in 1928, organismic theories emerged in other fields
as well. The new organismic conception was reflected in
the works of Cassirer (the philosophy of symbolic forms),
Piaget (language and learning), and Goldstein (biology and
neurophysiology). The organismic viewpoint opposed the
mechanistic orientation which emphasized parts and processes
rather than wholes, and the organizing relationships among the
parts in a "holistic" orientation. Bertalanffy believed that
living organisms are organized entities and that the biologist
must deal with them as such. Organismic theory emphasized
the notion that the analytic method of physics was not suited
to the problems of a living organism or a society. In other
words, the organismic theory "introduced concepts which
embody irreducible wholes in place of physically measurable
variables" (70, p. xvii). [9]

In 1929 Bertalanffy first presented the theory of open
systems, the second major precursor of general systems

theory, although he did not publish this until 1945.[10] At
that time the intellectual climate in the scientific world had
changed considerably from the earlier classical mechanistic
approach and there was considerable interest in model building and abstract generalizations in a number of scientific
fields.

The subject of open systems has received considerable
attention in almost all disciplines; just as there was wide
acceptance and utilization of the concept of system and the
organismic viewpoint, open system theory received almost
universal acclaim for advancing the state of science and
opening new paths and directions to the professional disciplines.   Some of the key concepts and principles of open
systems theory are briefly reviewed here.   Parallel developments in scientific fields are also cited, especially as these
provide the springboard for the subsequent analysis of selected issues and trends.

Open system theory is rooted in the idea of system-
environment exchange.   This was viewed by Bertalanffy in
relation to living, animate systems in contrast to inanimate
or closed systems.   The open system is associated with the
notion of the hierarchical order of systems, the relations
within and between subsystems (and components), systems,
and suprasystems, and the utilization of intersystem generalizations.   The latter are based on isomorphisms or
homomorphisms, and the search for these formal identities
between systems or theories of systems became a fulcrum
for general system theorists and general systems research.

Because open systems can import and utilize matter-
energy and information from their environments, they have
innate capacities for growth and elaboration and are capable

of increasing differentiation and specialization. The theory
of open systems thus resolved the apparent contradiction
between entropy and evolution. [11] Closed systems are characterized by increasing entropy, that is, increasing disorder
and de-differentiation. The import of negative entropy
permits open systems to maintain themselves at a high level
and evolve toward increasing states of order and complexity.

The concept of steady state and the principle of equifinality are key aspects of open system theory interrelated
with the notions of system levels, system-environment
exchange, and negentropy. They refute the assumption of
vitalists that living organisms follow different laws than the
laws of mechanical or closed systems and thereby became
more organized instead of disorganized. [12] In other words,
the maintenance of nonequilibrium states in living systems
is explained by the theory of open systems. Since there are
continually altering fluxes of matter-energy and information
in open systems, they tend to attain a steady state rather
than a static, unchanging equilibrium. Much has been
written about the distinctions between the concepts of equilibrium and steady state. While to some extent this may
be due to semantic differences, when examined more closely
in the light of the theoretical model and value orientation,
underlying questions and issues (not always made explicit)
are revealed. That is, one's scientific and value orientations with respect to stability and change (its form and
direction), man's relationship to nature and distinctions between human and nonhuman life, between organismic and
social systems, between simple-primitive and complex behavioral systems (in man and other living systems) shape
both the selection and meaning of concepts. Connections

between terminology and theory-value model are interwoven
into the totality of this book, but will be given particular
attention in later chapters.[13]

The steady state of open systems is characterized
by the principle of equifinality, which means achieving
identical results from different initial conditions. If a
system is open it can be shown that

> ... the final state will not depend on the initial
> concentrations but will be determined entirely by
> the properties of the system itself, that is, the
> constants of proportionality which are independent
> of the conditions imposed on the system. Such a
> system will appear to exhibit 'equifinality' or,
> metaphorically speaking, to have a 'goal of its
> own' [70, p. xviii].

It may be said, therefore, that the principle of equifinality
characteristic of open systems resolved the mechanistic-
vitalistic conflict. It brought the notion of system purpose or goal into the realm of modern science without
recourse to vitalistic or teleogical interpretation.[14]

While there is general consensus regarding the significance and usefulness of the principle of equifinality,
some system theorists have supplemented Bertalanffy's conception. For example, Miller and also Rapoport make the
important point that not only living but some nonliving or
inanimate systems are open and these acquire some of the
properties of living systems, such as equifinality (58, p. 125;
70, pp. xviii-xx). Bertalanffy's emphasis on the distinctions
rather than similarities or common features between living
and nonliving systems is reflected in his scientific-value
orientation, his theoretical model of man, and his analysis
of parallel theoretical developments. Additional supplements to Bertalanffy's principle of equifinality also concern

parallel theories and the system model. (See pp. 16-19 for
further elaboration and clarification.) Thus Miller concurs
with Bertalanffy's view of steady states of open systems being
dependent upon system constants more than environmental conditions; however, he points out that inputs outside the "normal" range may destroy the system or affect its structure
and functioning. Moreover, each system has its own individual history and therefore any final state is affected by
the various preceding genetic and environmental influences
which have impinged upon the system. As a result of their
histories, living systems may develop differently and have
different final characteristics (58, p. 125). Buckley, a
sociologist, writes in a vein similar to Miller's, and also
suggests the use of "an opposite principle [to equifinality]
called multifinality." The latter means that similar conditions may lead to dissimilar end-states. Buckley continues
to discuss multifinality in the context of a psycho-social
system model and notions of causality. He states, thus,
that "initial conditions in either the personality or the environment may or may not be relevant or causally dominant
(19, pp. 60-61).

The goal-directed open system is characterized by
a steady state (or dynamic equilibrium), as discussed above,
and also by inherent properties of stress[15] and strain.
When the system's variables are forced beyond their range
of stability, stress occurs and produces strain in the system
(58, p. 110). Tension (often used interchangeably with the
terms stress and strain) is believed by all systems theorists
to be a constant, inherent characteristic that does not occur
only occasionally or residually as a disturbing factor (19,
p. 28). The explanation of the nature and source of the

open system's steady state, stress and strain (or tension)
is based upon the theoretician's system model, e. g. , the
source of system tension may be due to its composition of
matter-energy, changes in the external environment or in
the system's structure, etc. Stress, strain, or tension are
often viewed in terms of their positive or negative values[16]--
i. e. , either producing growth and change or disorganization
and disruption of the system. It is generally accepted that
the open system's adjustment processes cope with stress
and strains and serve to maintain the system's stability and
integrity while simultaneously permitting system growth
and change. However, there are significant differences in
conceptions of adjustment processes or adaptation--de-
pending upon the theoretical model employed.

In Bertalanffy's theory of open systems the primary
processes of self-regulation and goal-directiveness are those
of the dynamic interaction of system parts and processes.
This dynamic interaction in the system not only re-establishes
its steady state but enables the system to evolve toward increasing differentiation, inhomogeneity, and specialization.
Secondary regulatory mechanisms governed by fixed structures are subsequently superimposed upon this basic dynamic
regulation by way of "progressive mechanization. " Bertalanffy stresses thus, that in development and evolution,
dynamic interaction (in the open system) precedes mechanization (structured arrangements) which impose constraints
upon the system. [17] According to this view (Bertalanffy),
general systems theory is considered the more general and
encompassing theory overarching parallel theoretical developments in other fields--i. e. , other systems theories.
Bertalanffy states that his general systems theory is a

model of only certain aspects of reality and he believes
there is need for additional models for other aspects of
reality. Nevertheless, he concludes that "general systems
theory can logically be considered the more general theory":
other systems theories "are but a rather restricted subclass of 'general systems'" (12, pp. 16, 19, 37). Other
systems theorists take a somewhat different position with
respect to the relationship between general systems theory
(open system theory) and parallel or subsequent developments in the realm of systems sciences and systems theories.
For example, open systems are often depicted as "control"
systems based upon transmission processes within and between systems, or as information-processing systems. In
some ways, the latter type of system model is overlapping
and compatible with general systems theory; in other ways
it modifies, supplements, or supplants Bertalanffy's open
system and general systems formulations.

Parallel Theories

The impetus for parallel theoretical developments
in scientific and applied fields originated in the new complex
technology, part of the Second Industrial Revolution. While
the First Industrial Revolution contributed the principle of
transformation of energy from one form to another, the
Second dealt with the machines that processed large amounts
of information and were capable of appropriate, "purposeful"
decision-making. As Rapoport states,

> ... the appearance of complex information-process-
> ing machines suggested a new concept of the living
> organism, ... in addition to being an engine
> (transformation of energy) and a chemical labora-
> tory (transformation of matter), [it] was also a
> decision-making system (a device for processing,

storing, and retrieving information) [70, p. xx].

As this new model of the living organism was found to have validity and utility, the distinctions between living and non-living systems became less meaningful. The common features of living and nonliving systems derive from the way systems are organized. The generalization of organism to organized system is crucial to various developments in systems theories and systems research (see 70, p. xx).

A number of theories are described as parallel developments to general systems theory. The selections and definitions of these, however, as well as their status as precursors, parallel, or subsequent theoretical developments, are varied and debatable. Bertalanffy cites the commonalities and differences among parallel theoretical developments; the former are their concern with behavioral and biological sciences, use of models different from that of physics, and their interdisciplinary nature; the latter are their model conceptions and their mathematical methods. He further notes, however, that these parallel developments "are not mutually exclusive and often combined in application" (12, p. 14). Whether these theories are overlapping and complementary, whether they share some common features while differing in others, the question remains whether they should be viewed as separate theories, particularistic theories within a global theory, theories integrated into general systems theory, or theories included "as part of the modern systems movement" (31, p. 20). Scanning the literature indicates that there are indeed "integrations" which are evidenced in the more recent publications of general systems theorists and researchers as well as those of discipline theorists.

Of some interest is the particular selection of and
rationale for theories designated as parallel to general
systems theory. Bertalanffy distinguishes between theories
of basic systems sciences and theories of "applied systems
sciences ... which are closely connected with modern auto-
mation." Thus, he views operations research, systems
engineering, and human engineering as applied systems
sciences and cybernetics, information theory, game theory,
decision theory, topology (relational mathematics), factor
analysis, and general system theory (in the narrow sense)
as the theories of basic systems sciences. Other writers
do not use this type of theory-differentiation; however, the
way in which the theories are classified (partly determined
by the scientific-professional orientation) also influences the
way in which they are defined. Gray and Rizzo, "systems
theory psychiatrists," offer a long list of parallel theories,
similar to Bertalanffy's, but they elaborate on only three:
operations research, cybernetics, and gestalt psychology
(which is not even mentioned by Bertalanffy). Whereas
operations research is presented as the scientific control of
existing systems of men, machines, materials, and money
by Bertalanffy, Gray and Rizzo discuss operations research
as a method of unifying sciences which is applied in the
inventory processes of business and industry.

Cybernetics and information (and communication)
theories probably have had the greatest impact on all fields
--basic or applied; although they are separate theory-models,
to varying degrees, they have also been integrated into general systems theory. A few observations at this point about
theories of cybernetics and information-communication are
relevant to understanding the advances in systems theory,

and (as noted in Part III) the ways in which they have been
utilized to update and/or change certain discipline theories.

<u>Control Systems: Feedback Model and Systems Model</u>

All definitions of cybernetics cite it as a model of
control systems.   Rapoport states that

> ... it examines patterns of signals by means of
> which information is transmitted within a system
> and from one system to another.   Transmission
> of information is essential in control and the capa-
> city of a system to exercise control depends on
> how much information it can process and store.
> In fact, the concept of 'quantity of information' is
> central to cybernetics [70, p. xix].

Thus cybernetics is concerned with the quantity rather than
the meaning of the information, and the quantity of information is related to the number of decisions which must be
made, or, stated differently, to the reduction of uncertainty.
Bertalanffy and others emphasize the key explanatory
mechanism of cybernetics--"feedback or circular causal
trains providing mechanisms for goal-seeking and self-con-
trolling behavior" (12, p. 13).   Wiener, the "founder" of
cybernetics, as well as others such as Rapoport, Ashby,
and Miller, writes of cybernetics as applicable to both the
animal and the machine, the nonliving and living systems,
thereby leading to the recognition of formal identities among
these various sorts of systems.   Three aspects of cybernetics should be underscored: 1) its utility in decision-
making (reducing uncertainty and making choices, both of
which are involved in adjustment processes and adaptation);
2) its utility in establishing isomorphisms among system
levels; 3) the provision of "a set of concepts susceptible to
logical (or mathematical) operations, from which 'purposeful'

or 'intelligent' aspects of living systems could be derived"
(70, pp. xix-xx).

The study of methods of feedback control is viewed
by many theorists and practitioners as a basic notion of
systems theory. Feedback "refers to some of the consequences of outputs--consequences which are fed back into
the input and processing to affect succeeding outputs" (48,
p. 52). There appear to be two basic differences among
theorists, however, regarding the feedback model. As
suggested above (p. 15-16), Bertalanffy views the feedback
scheme as represented by the concept of homeostasis in the
living organism and thus a restricted subclass of general
systems theory. Whereas cybernetics is devoted to the study
of feedback arrangements, Bertalanffy states that GST and
open system theory are primarily concerned with the dynamic
interaction within multivariable systems. In essence then,
the feedback model and the open system model are different
representations of biological and behavioral phenomena.
According to Gray and Rizzo in their discussion of parallel
theoretical developments, gestalt psychology is very similar
to Bertalanffy's GST and open system theories.

> It stresses perhaps even more strongly that regu-
> lation is a property of the system as a whole,
> rather than a function of cybernetic controls which
> are considered secondary. It is not possible to
> conceive a gestalt except in the presence of
> dynamic regulation, in the same way that it is
> not possible to conceive of an integrated system
> without the presence of dynamic regulation in such
> forms as steady states and equifinality [31, p. 23]. 18

Wiener, Buckley, Vickers, and others offer a broader
perspective of the feedback mechanism. Wiener defines feedback as the

> ... property of being able to adjust future conduct
> by past performance. It may be simple as the
> common reflex, or it may be a higher order feed-
> back, in which past experience is used not only
> to regulate specific movements, but also whole
> policies of behavior. Such a policy-feedback may,
> and often does, appear to be what we know under
> one aspect as conditioned reflex, and under an-
> other as learning [96, p. 33].

The latter orientation to feedback plays a significant role in
both the application of systems theory and in current theoretical developments. Feedback thus may be viewed as
some predetermined internal mechanism that aims blindly
in system self-regulation, or it may be viewed as directing
the behavior of the system in goal-directed and not merely
goal-oriented ways. This is of particular interest in understanding and dealing with the evolution of complex adaptive
systems. As Buckley states,

> ... our concern is not so much with homeostatic
> mechanisms, which may or may not be made
> more comprehensible by translation into feedback
> terms, but rather with mechanisms that direct
> system behavior. These latter mechanisms run
> the gamut from tropistic, instinctual, and reflexive
> feedback testing mechanisms, to learned, conscious,
> symbol-actuated subsystems, to the mechanisms of
> social planning [19, p. 53].

Goal-setting and goal-direction of systems are based
upon the correction of error or deviations from the goal-
state. This in turn relates to the notions of negative and
positive feedback. The former maintains the steady state
of the system while the latter alters the variables of the
system and destroys the steady state. Thus positive feedback can initiate system changes--if, however, it continues
and is unlimited it may destroy the system. Amplification
feedback may operate in both negative and positive feedback.

Amplification feedback (e.g., chain reaction) and feedback
loops have contributed to notions of structure-building in
systems and in causal analysis of system change. The deviation-amplifying process challenges the unidirectional cause
and effect analysis. Rapoport has argued for "explanation in
terms of 'efficient' causes operating here and now, and not
of 'final' causes. ... We can treat 'purpose' causally in
the former sense of forces acting here and now; if we can
build a model of purposefulness, we can explain it" (Rapoport quoted by Buckley, 19, p. 52).[19]

A few remarks on information-communication theory
conclude this section of the chapter devoted to general systems theory and its parallel theoretical developments.
Modern information theory focuses on the fundamental nature
of the mediating linkage underlying the interrelations and
interactions in complex adaptive systems. The goal-seeking
characteristics of such open systems depend on the particular
character of information and the process of its communication within systems and between systems and their environments (including other systems). One aspect of information
theory deals with "the abstract logical nature of information,
its mathematical measure and its close affinity with the
notions of structure, organization, control, order, and
entropy" (20, p. 119). Information theory is also concerned
with the phenomenon of meaning, which is a distinguishing
characteristic of the human mind (its capacity to manipulate
symbols), and its generation out of social interactions. Information theory thus provides key explanatory concepts for
the phenomenon of system-environment adaptation. That is,
it is the nature of the system-environment interchanges
that make possible the "mapping" of the system's informa-

tion pool into the system's structure.

> It is such mappings [both of the organism-system
> and its environment] that make possible the
> system's control of its behavior in ways relevant
> to or coordinate with the nature of its environ-
> ment such that, in effect, system and environment
> become interacting components of a larger whole.
> Such a conceptualization provides a common prin-
> ciple for the otherwise diverse facts of phylo-
> genetic evolution, ontogenetic development, psycho-
> logical learning, or sociocultural elaboration [20,
> p. 119].

Information, in this context, is understood foremost as a
relation or mapping (of information) and performs a selective function on the system's behavior. "Something is
selected from a well-defined set. To examine the selective
process, it is essential to be able to examine the set" (71,
p. 139). Since information is "relational" the meaning does
not reside in the signals transmitted but is instead a function
of the larger system and the relevant environments. Buckley
points out that this is "a crucial foundation for the transactional view of the nature of all open behavioral systems"
(20, p. 121).

In addition to examining information theory in terms
of the transmission processes (e.g., information coding)
and semantics or the meaning of information, the pragmatics
of information theory is of considerable interest to theoreticians and practitioners. Thus information theorists have
focused upon the behavior of communicatively interacting
human beings. A model of the communicative behavior of
two or more individuals explains "how transmitted information selectively links mind to mind and makes possible co-
ordinate, mutually influenced behaviors" (20, p. 122). It
is clear then that information-communication theory covers

a wide range of concepts and principles that significantly contribute to systems theory, its extensions and applications. In sum, parallel theoretical developments to general systems theory, especially the theories of cybernetics and information-communication, have led to changes in definitions of systems, their concepts and processes. The basic notions of steady state, stress and strain, as well as system regulation and adaptation (goal-correction and goal-setting) are cast in terms of transmission processes within and between systems, e. g., input, throughput, output, and feedback. And finally, notions of system structure, function, and history, hierarchical system levels, and system-environment relations are clarified and connected to modern scientific theory.

NOTES FOR PART I

1. Extensive bibliographies on systems theory are available and accessible. This writer has written on systems theory and its application to social work practice (see 88, 89).

2. The role of language and terminology will appear and reappear as an integral part of the whole book.

3. There will be further consideration in this chapter regarding the subject of system levels; it is referred to here and will be elaborated upon in the discussion of general systems theory and its applications.

4. The term epigenetic comes from the field of biology. Erikson applied the term to his personality theory of psycho-social development. In this sense, epigenetics is the ground plan for the sequential stages of development.

5. Chin distinguishes between empirical and analytic or conceptual systems, whereas Miller distinguishes between concrete, abstracted, and conceptual systems.

6. Miller defines the boundary of a system as "that re-
    gion where greater energy is required for trans-
    mission across it than for transmission immediately
    outside that region or immediately inside it" (57,
    pp. 516-517).

7. R. W. Gerard, "Becoming: The Residue of Change," in
    S. Tax (ed.), The Evolution of Man, Vol. II,
    Chicago, University of Chicago Press, 1960, p.
    255 (quoted by Miller in Gray, 58; from hence on,
    unless otherwise noted, 58 will refer to Miller in
    Gray). As stated above, there will be further
    consideration of the terms of structure, function,
    and process. However it might be noted here that
    this writer has been impressed by the current
    trend, especially noted among social scientists,
    of dispensing with the concept of structure and
    giving primary emphasis to the concept of process.

8. The subject of system levels is fully considered by
    Miller, who distinguishes seven levels of living
    systems and differentiates between suprasystems,
    systems, and subsystems. He recognizes that
    his distinction of seven levels is arbitrary. He
    justifies the distinction of system levels as derived
    from a long scientific tradition of empirical obser-
    vation (58, p. 91).

9. See references to the organismic theory-model in
    Parts II and III.

10. During the 1930's, however, Bertalanffy continued his
    work on open systems theory, elaborating on his
    initial formulations.

11. The disorder, disorganization, lack of patterning, or
    randomness of organization of a system is known
    as its entropy. Living systems can avoid an in-
    crease in entropy (characteristic of closed systems)
    through the import of energy and information.
    Thus it has been said that "life feeds on negative
    entropy" (20, p. 140). Subsequently, the im-
    portant relationship between information and entropy
    was explored; for example, it has been found that
    the statistical measure for the negative of entropy
    is the same as that for information-negentropy.
    It is obvious then that the concept of entropy is of

significance in open system theory and has been
cited as a guiding concept for social work practice.
(See subsequent discussion in the chapters on applications of systems theory.)

12. Vitalists believe that the processes of life are not
     explicable by the laws of physics and chemistry
     alone and that life is in some part self-determining
     instead of mechanistically determined.

13. Distinctions and differences in use of concepts and
     terminology appear in writings of Allport, Ber-
     talanffy, Bowlby, Buckley, etc. Of particular
     interest are declarations of opposing views which
     are based solely on one author's interpretation of
     another author's position or viewpoint.

14. Teleology has been defined as the philosophical study
     of evidence of design in nature. In different
     terms, final states or ends are considered im-
     manent in nature. Phenomena and events are
     explained by final cause or by the design of a
     divine providence.

15. Selye, as a biologist and theoretician, did original
     and major work in applying the concept of stress
     to living systems at the organism level (81).

16. This subject is given considerable attention in the lit-
     erature. (See for example, The Functions of Con-
     flict by Lewis Coser, which emphasizes the posi-
     tive nature of conflict in establishing unity or re-
     establishing unity and cohesion in a system. The
     positive values of system stress, strain, or tension
     frequently appear in discussions of system theory
     applications (89, pp. 171-172).

17. See pp. 102-106 in Part III for additional comments on
     self-regulation and homeostasis of systems.

18. In his book, Structuralism, Piaget states that "gestalt
     psychology is ... a structuralist theory more on
     account of its use of equilibration principles than
     because of the laws of wholeness it proposes"
     (67, pp. 56-57).

19.   If prior events are proximal to the event being ex-
       plained, we refer to "efficient causes"; if more
       distant, we refer to "historical causes" (as quoted
       by Stein, 89, p. 187).

PART II

APPLICATIONS

This section and the following one (Part III) are closely intertwined: this section deals with the current applications and utilizations of systems theory in social work and psychiatry; the next section deals with the "changing faces" of theory--old and new, concepts and semantics. The different perspectives and foci encompassed in these discussions may enhance the reader's understanding of the primary concern of this book, namely, trends and issues in systems theory.

Chapter 2

SYSTEMS THEORY AND SOCIAL WORK

INTRODUCTION: BACKGROUND

The subject of systems theory and its relationship to
social work practice has been given considerable attention
since the late 1950's. This is evidenced by the substantial
number of publications as well as papers delivered at pro-
fessional-educational conferences. [1] In the 1940's and the
early 1950's similar attention was given to particular sociological concepts and social system theory. The latter was
a positive response to the new developments in the social
sciences and simultaneously a "counter" response to social
work's traditional preoccupation with and adherence to
psychiatric (and more specifically psychoanalytic) theory.

Rather than reiterate or supplement available materials, the application of systems theory will be presented
here in the form of a re-view and analysis. First, however,
it is important to point out that the subject of applications
requires that the scope and nature of the practice interventions be examined in light of their relationship to theory;
it also requires that the theory be examined in light of
practice interventions. While the primary focus is upon the
application of systems theory to social work, it is useful to
draw some comparisons with psychiatry and the impact of
systems theory on its practices and theoretical constructs.

The literature reveals that the application of systems

theory to social work has been approached from the two
perspectives cited: from practice to theory and from theory
to practice. [2] Both perspectives are valid and necessary.
However, misconceptions and confusions in thinking tend to
occur when authors' conflicting or incongruent professional
value orientations and conceptual constructs are employed
simultaneously or in combination, when distinctions between
different levels of scientific explanation are not noted or
clarified and are masked by the use of inappropriate terminology. Stated differently, the literature on the applications of systems theory to social work indicates that different
theories are often equated with or substituted for each other,
that empirical experiences are often equated with scientific
constructs, that conceptual models and notions are conveyed
in, or interwoven with, the "language of persons" and the
language and ideology of the profession.

This subject will be amplified in later discussion;[3]
one illustration is cited here. Starting with the "given"--
namely, the variety and range of social work practice
interventions in different system levels--one author views
systems theory as providing the appropriate context and
rationale for these interventions and their implementation.
Another author starts with the "given"--namely, systems
theory concepts--then points out ways in which they suggest
new types of social work interventions and roles. The latter are inferential and based upon the author's ideological
stance, particular concepts selected, and limited use of
relevant research. Comparison of the two approaches reveals
basic differences in utilization of systems theory and in value
orientations leading to opposing or antithetical notions of
social work practice.

A number of recurrent themes in social work literature on systems theory can be identified. It may then be
possible to consider: first, whether there is evidence of a
shift in the themes or emphases in the past decade; second,
what conclusions, implications, and questions are suggested;
third, a comparison with some materials in the psychiatric
literature on systems theory.

One general basic theme in the social work literature
highlights the compatibility of social work concepts and social
work values with systems theory. In different terms,
traditional social work concepts can be translated into
systems concepts; in demonstrating the compatibility via
translation, social work concepts are validated and rein-
forced with enhanced meaning. Systems theory gives social
work the conceptual tools to explain long-standing notions
and to guide and give direction to social work practice.

The most frequently cited social work concept is the
person-situation configuration and the psycho-social nature
of all social work practice. The interrelatedness and the
interdependence of the person and his environment may
easily be understood in the context of open system theory;
e.g., the interchange of energy and information between
the system and its environment, whereby the system maintains a steady state, may develop increasing complexity and
specialization (negentropy), may achieve the same ends from
varying initial conditions (equifinality). A change in the
system affects the environment and vice versa. Thus, such
explanatory concepts of the system-environment relationship
made it possible to overcome the dichotomization between
the system and environment which had been a "persistent
pattern in social work practice" (84, p. 75). In other

words, it "dissolved the hyphen between system and environment" since in reality they are parts of a whole--"a system together with its environment makes up the universe of all things of interest in a given context" (37, pp. 83-84).
Other social work practice concepts and principles clarified by systems theory include the process of individualization, the worker-client relationship, the client's participation, and the worker's self-awareness. Individualization is understood in the context of the systems of which the client is a part and which affect him. Understanding the helping organization as a system and the worker and client as part of that system provides a broader context for change in the client-system, the helping system and other social (environment) systems. [4]
The client's active (oppositional) participation in the helping system and other societal institutions, as well as the worker's boundary-maintaining (social control) function, expands the traditional concepts of the worker-client relationship and the worker's self-awareness.

Another central theme is the compatibility of systems theory with long-standing values of social work. The latter include: the uniqueness of and respect for the individual, his self-determination and innate potentialities for creativity and self-direction (40, 41, 48, 49, 84). These core social work values are consonant with open system theory, especially its concepts of steady state, dynamic processes of system self-regulation, system-environment exchange and interdependence and, most importantly, the principle of equifinality. Open system theory thus explains and supports social work's belief in the creativity of man and his capacity for growth and development, as well as his ability to shape his own destiny and influence his environment.

The literature discussed above focuses on social
work concepts and values and the ways in which they are
explained "scientifically" when translated into systems theory
terms. Some of the literature, however, focuses on systems
concepts selectively, stressing the utility of particular concepts in clarifying and implementing change processes, interventive approaches and techniques. The concept (or
concepts) chosen--for example, system boundary, tension
and conflict, feedback and feedback loop--reflects the author's
interest and experience in certain types of practice interventions, as well as his professional values and training. [5]

The literature highlights a third major focus of interest and concern. Systems theory has been viewed as the
key to a holistic conception of social work practice, the
development of social work "generalists," and a unified
theory of social work. The search for a basic conception
of social work began with Hearn's initial publication on
theory-building (40); it was continued by other social work
theorists and educators (using different approaches) as general systems theory itself was elaborated, refined, and
debated. Two approaches to building a unified social work
theory (similar to the two approaches to general systems
theory, see pp. 9-10) are the analogistic (empirico-intuitive)
and the generic (deductive) (39). These approaches are
rooted in: one, the notion of hierarchy of system levels
(and the application of cross-level propositions); two, the
notion of master models applicable to all systems of social
work practice. [6]

The analogistic approach to the unification of social
work theory and practice was demonstrated by "experiments"
in social work education--field and academic curricula (82,

83). Master models proposed for social work are based
upon somewhat different orientations to systems theory and
social work although it is possible to identify certain convergences and similarities. Gordon's model is based on the
system concept of entropy and the system notion of transaction and exchange between system and environment (30).
Polsky's model utilizes the functional-dysfunctional analysis
of Parsonian social system theory. This analysis deals
primarily with the relationship between the client system,
the helping system, and societal systems (68). Lathrope's
paradigm (as a master model) is built around the information-processing model--input, processing, output, and feedback. The analogistic approach and the master models[7]
reveal some commonalities: e.g., increasing attention to
activities in the boundary region between systems, the
utility of information theory (especially information-processing
and feedback), and the conceptualization of system-environment interdependence in terms of their "matching" so that
both system and environment are benefited and enhanced.[8]
Finally, it is important to note that both the analogistic
approach and the master models proposed are applicable to
social work with individuals, families, groups, and community systems. In sum, the significance of systems theory
for social work at this time was seen as providing a theoretical framework which could bridge and integrate the range
of knowledge from various fields (biological, psychological,
social, and cultural). This conceptual framework was expected to advance and unify social work theory and practice
resulting in the dissolution of traditional method compartmentalizations.

CURRENT THEORETICAL CONCEPTIONS
AND OPERATIONAL INTERPRETATIONS

Within the past few years there are indications in
the literature that the utilization or application of systems
theory has been, and perhaps is continuing to be, modified.
While there is tacit acceptance of systems theory generally, close scrutiny reveals some differences that have
significance. As might be expected, these differences reflect the change and ferment characteristic of our complex
modern world. That is, the changes and modifications
identified in the social work literature are not isolated or
limited to the social work profession. Nevertheless, the
nature of these changes and the sources or reasons for their
occurrence deserve attention.

The basic shift is in the movement away from general
systems theory as a "well-formed theoretical framework"
(6, p. 374). Instead, systems theory has become a context,
a rationale, a way of thinking, an operational style. The
concept of system and parts of general systems theory continue to be used selectively, with some modifications, and in
interesting combinations with other conceptual constructs or
theories. It is the totality of these particular shifts, additions, and combinations which reflects the "state" of the
social work field, as well as its dilemmas and solutions.
Aspects of systems theory which are still in "favor," those
that have been "rejected," and other constructs and orientations which have been utilized as additions or replacements
will be identified.

The main theme or thesis this trend represents (for
this writer) is the "turning away" from efforts toward a
serious, systematic, rigorous investigation of the

developments in science and their import for professional
disciplines, including social work. While the shift with
regard to systems theory may, at first glance, seem "for-
ward-looking," there may be drawbacks or limitations which
must also be considered by social work theoreticians and
practitioners. Instead of updating our body of scientific
knowledge and underpinnings and testing concepts for their
validity and utility, it is possible that we have settled upon
an easier path to pursue. If our perspective from this new
path appears to be wider and more attractive, it also raises
questions about its logical grounding, its coherence and integrity, its directions and implications for the social work
profession in our "complex, rapidly-changing, modern world."

    Current literature suggests that the notion of system
as a whole with interrelated parts that affect each other and
the whole, and also the basic concepts and principles encompassed by open system theory, are still perceived as
valid. By and large, however, they are utilized selectively
and are often removed from their theoretical context and
given somewhat different emphases, especially when combined with other constructs or other theoretical orientations.
For example, the import of the nature of the relationships
of the parts (their organization and patterning) is useful to
family system theoreticians and practitioners. The latter,
however, draw upon selected aspects of information and
communication theories as their explanatory conceptual tools
and guides for their specific and preferred practice interventions. Social workers are familiar with various notions
of communication problems, e.g., stereotyped patterns of
interchange, overload of input stimuli, double-bind messages,
gaps or distortions in feedback, characteristic of "sick"

family systems. (See pp. 46-48 for additional comments regarding operational interpretations of communication theory.)

The ways in which information and communication theories are selectively utilized suggest that social workers often do not fully comprehend the meaning of the particular concept employed. In a recent publication, Meyer discusses the feedback process "where energy is imported into the system." She further states that "the theory accounts for the effect upon the system of the new source of energy, where the existing status of the system becomes transformed through the transactions of the person-family-environmental systems" (56, p. 133). While it is certainly true that both energy and information are incorporated in the flow of information--that is, input, processing, output, and feedback--the feedback model (developed within cybernetic theory) is concerned solely with the nature and transmission of information rather than energy. It is the transformation of information that is the keynote of information theory, of negative and positive feedback, of the deviation-amplifying process. (See for example, 66, especially pp. 91-105.) Moreover, the transformation cited by Meyer not only refers to energy, rather than information, [9] but it is placed in the context of "transaction." Meyer, thus, has interwoven her discussion of systems theory with the feedback process and with the notion of transaction. The transactional framework appears to be the primary basis for Meyer's analysis of social work practice and theory. Since other authors have also brought the notion of "transactional field" to the forefront of social work, it will be discussed briefly at a later point.

A final word about feedback is pertinent here.   The
debate about the "place" of feedback in systems theory (noted
in the earlier section on general systems theory) may not
be fully recognized by current social work authors.   Two
positions may justifiably be taken: feedback as a basic
model for living as well as nonliving systems (Wiener,
Rapoport, etc.) or the open system model with feedback
as a secondary regulatory, homeostatic mechanism imposing
constraints on the basic dynamic interaction processes
(Bertalanffy, Allport, etc.).   Thus, the author needs to
make explicit his definition of the concept, its theoretical
basis, and its use as a model.   This writer suspects
that social workers, being "eclectic," probably employ both
the feedback concept and concepts of open system theory,
but they do not always clarify the concepts, the ways in
which they are combined, and/or are logically interrelated.
Certainly, most social work authors, as well as authors
from other disciplines, would concur with general systems
theorists that multi-variable open systems are "beyond homeostasis" (16, p. 40).   It is now fairly well accepted that
this concept or model (homeostasis) has been expanded to
considerations of steady state and heterostasis.

Open system theory continues thus to be viewed as
valid and useful--although, as noted, there are some confusions or misconceptions in the understanding and application of selected open system concepts.   However, another
basic tenet of general systems theory, the hierarchy of
system levels, is currently questioned or debated by some
social work authors, as well as by authors from other disciplines.   Nevertheless, the notion of system levels often
provides the framework for translation and analysis of

generic systems concepts, e. g. , structure, [10] as well as
concepts borrowed from other theories (sometimes sub-
sumed under systems theory).

The "psychic structure" of psychoanalytic theory is
frequently cited as a translation of systems theory structure at the personality level. Unfortunately, this is of no
service to psychoanalytic theory (see Part III on Changing
Faces of Theory) or to systems theory. It is especially
true when the translation is presented in the context of
the compatibility of social work and systems theory (and by
implication the validation and support of traditional social
work theory and practice) (41). It is also true when the
translation involves misunderstanding or misuse of concepts
of psychic structure, e. g. , the ego, [11] and when translation
is offered merely as a "token" acceptance of psychoanalytic
theory. Thus, Freudian psychoanalytic concepts may be
translated into systems terms, but other preferred personality and behavior theories also can be and are being translated into systems terms.

Crisis theory and crisis intervention are popular sub-
jects in the social work literature. While the notion of
crisis did not emerge as a concept within general systems
theory nor as one of the parallel theories to systems theory,
a number of authors have indicated that it is compatible with
systems concepts. Crisis has been defined as "an upset in
a steady state" and thus crisis "treatment" or crisis intervention in social work is directed toward the reestablish-
ment of the steady state (72, pp. 21-31; 56, p. 176).

Discussions of crisis theory include the notion of
system levels, the theoretical constructs on which it is
based or with which it is combined, as well as its operational

interpretations. First, "crisis" has been identified and described in biological, personality, family, group, and community systems. Theoreticians and practitioners, thus, from different fields or disciplines have contributed to crisis theory as it relates to physiological states and symptoms (Selye), personality development (Erikson), natural life situations, e. g., bereavement (Lindemann), family life cycle (Rapoport, Rhona; Haley; et al.), urban redevelopment, and disasters and epidemics in communities. Second, while crisis theory was developed by theoreticians and practitioners working at many system levels, most social work authors refer to its theoretical origins in ego psychology, stress, and role "theories." Their writings emphasize the ego's functions of coping and mastery and resolution of role discomplementarities and conflicts, especially in the context of developmental tasks and family relationships. Third, crisis theory, when viewed in terms of the person and his situation (i. e., subjective and objective influences), has been defined as "transactional theory," or "a system of interweaving forces, all having reciprocity and feedback with each other" (56, pp. 180, 123).

The above discussion has dealt with the notion of system levels and systems theory translations as they apply to other constructs and theories such as psychoanalytic theory, ego psychology, role concepts, crisis theory and transactional theory. Although selective aspects of information and communication theories are given some attention in the social work literature, e. g., communication patterns in "sick" families, a more systematic and comprehensive knowledge of these theories may, hopefully, lead to renewed interest in broader scientific theory, its connections with other theories, and its import for the future of the social work profession.

Finally, the operational interpretations of the notion of system levels and related constructs and theories hold great interest for the practice intervention-oriented worker. It would be impossible as well as impractical to summarize the range and variety of social work writings devoted to this subject. However, some illustrative points regarding crisis theory intervention writings appear to be pertinent and significant. Beginning in the late 1950's and early 1960's social work was interested in and gravitating toward a normal or healthy developmental frame of reference, away from an earlier focus on abnormal development and pathology.[12] Thus, notions of developmental, maturational, "natural life," and situational crises make it possible for social workers to move into wider fields, collaborate with other disciplines, and utilize innovative intervention techniques.

The concept of crisis, by definition, is time-limited and characterized by typical, identifiable phases and behaviors (e.g., rise in tension, impairment in social functioning, cognitive confusion, feelings of helplessness and desire for help). "Healthy" crisis resolution by social workers requires knowledge of the "temporal and phasic aspects" of crises, as well as skill in use of available resources, rapid appraisal of precipitating stress factors, management of tension discharge, techniques of clarification and cognitive restructuring of the problem-situation, and development of appropriate and/or new coping mechanisms and adaptive patterns. The goal in crisis intervention is not to achieve insight into, or cure of, intrapsychic conflicts

but is the restoration of ego-role functioning, the reestab-
lishment of the "system's" steady state, and the prevention
of disorganization or breakdown. Crisis intervention may
also lead to a new steady state at a higher level and with a
wider range of coping-adaptive patterns. Although Meyer
disputes the validity of the notion of system levels, she
writes about crises as they occur in personality development,
families and communities; she states that "the practice model
of crisis intervention is ... partly public health and the interest in the early prevention of breakdown and partly community psychiatry and social casework with their recent attention to ego-functioning and coping capacities" (56, p. 178).

Crisis theory and crisis intervention have been connected to or equated with short-term and brief treatment
with individuals, families, and groups. Both (crisis intervention and brief treatment) share some common attributes:
for example, time-limits (number of interviews or numbers
of weeks/months), limited and/or specific goals (e.g., re-
establishment of the former steady state, reduction in impairment in functioning, change in identifiable, observable
behavior problems, etc.), increased direction and activity
in the worker's role. These similarities may be appealing
and attractive to practitioners, administrators, and policy-
planners. The obvious reasons are the time and economic
saving factors which make services available to more people
more rapidly. [13] Moreover, pilot programs, demonstrations,
and research "prove" that short-term and crisis treatment
result in greater improvement (according to specified outcome criteria) than long-term or continued-service treatment (74). Despite these impressive findings, significant
differences between crisis theory intervention and theories

of planned brief treatment should not be overlooked or
casually dismissed; clarification of conceptual models and
tools, professional goals, targets, and strategies is required.
Systems-information theory may be a useful framework to
guide an analysis of the process of change. Included in such
an analysis are: the structure and changing functions of
helping systems, the characteristics of the client-family
systems, as well as the "impinging environment" or societal
systems, the information-communication processing pattern
within and among the systems, and the set-goal or goal-
directedness of the systems as they are mutually interrelated in space and time.

The scope of this chapter does not permit such a full
analysis or discussion of the differences between short-term
treatment and crisis intervention. However, a few relevant
points and questions are in order. In the past decade, hos-
pitals, community health centers, and social agencies have
espoused and instituted "walk-in clinics" and "around-the-
clock" emergency health services. Are such forms of treatment and services rooted in the conceptual base (or model)
of crisis theory or in theories of brief psychotherapy?[14]
How do the client populations receiving emergency services
compare with the client populations offered and receiving
family therapy, crisis intervention, or group treatment?
Is behavior modification a form of planned short-term treatment; does it share the same conceptual model and tools,
treatment goals and techniques? The implication here is
simply that various types of treatment may be classified as
short-term but have important differences theoretically and
empirically. For example, emergency or brief psychotherapy may be oriented to "crisis" and draw on crisis

theory; on the other hand, it may be conceived within
learning theory, cybernetic theory, or the theory of "relational interaction" taken from the "moment-duration perspective" (90 and 66).

Social work literature has dealt with the relationship
between crisis theory intervention and the fields of public
health and mental health. For example, it is suggested that
the crisis model is the same as the public health model
(56). It might be useful, therefore, to inquire about the
compatibility of these models with the open system, information-processing, and feedback models. Whether the crisis
and public health models are indeed the same may be open
to question. However, they both appear to be middle-range
theories (selectively drawing on and combining abstract concepts) which are closer to empirical realities of interest to
social work and other professional disciplines. One common
feature refers to their focus on, or goal of, prevention
(primary or secondary), rather than "cure." Moreover, it
is suggested that the crisis model be applied to the community mental health as well as to the public health fields
(63). Crisis intervention in community mental health is
considered a form of primary prevention--"breakdown can
be avoided by the presence of timely help acting for a relatively short period of time" (21, pp. 186-187). These
statements indicate that concepts referable to one system
level are applied to other system levels. Thus, the goal
and/or target systems are depicted in terms of the individual or family system, although the implied goal-target
system is the community. In other words, the crisis model
of intervention seeks to reestablish a steady state of the
target system, namely, the individual or family. [15] The

public health model of intervention, however, seeks to pre-
vent illness or disease, and the community or "the population-at-large" is the target system. Primary prevention
seeks to alter or modify the environment-community. Where
this is infeasible or insufficient, methods of reducing sus-
ceptibility to the disease are introduced into the community,
"population-at-large" system. [16]

In sum, the development and application of crisis
theory intervention and numerous other "short-term services"
popularized in social work during the 1960's cannot be
divorced from prevailing concerns about the "deprofessional-
ization" of social work, social work's identity diffusion, the
search for new practice fields and arenas as well as new
tools, the concurrent changes taking place in other related
disciplines, the pervasive value conflicts and the dilemmas
of our "brave new world." It is this writer's thesis that
only in the context of greater knowledge of current scientific
theories and with careful scrutiny of conceptual values and
terminological factors can the social work profession determine its directions and arrive at some solutions to these
issues.

The above discussion focused on the operational interpretations of crisis theory as reflected in social work literature. It was pointed out that crisis theory is based upon
selected concepts from ego psychology and role "theory" and
that it combines these concepts with other concepts depending
upon the level of system in crisis and the environments of
which it is a part. As a middle-range theory it is closer to
empirical data of living systems than the abstract level of
general systems theory. Nevertheless, crisis theory is
frequently translated into systems terms for explanatory and

clarifying purposes: e.g., systems concepts of steady state, input overload, input and processing distortions, output "symptoms," positive feedback, feedback lags, etc.

Communication theory (often viewed as part of information theory) has been integrated into systems theory (e.g., 58, 70) and has been operationalized in practice by social work and other professional disciplines. Comparative analysis of the operational interpretations of communication theory is beyond the scope of this chapter but would be a most interesting and profitable subject for study. A wide variety of change strategies and interventions (including psychotherapy and family therapy) have been based upon limited, selective dimensions of communication theory.[17] Several concepts may be selected and combined in accord with the theoretician's/practitioner's frame of reference. The nature and consequences of communication patterns in families have been investigated with respect to the cognitive development of children, disturbances in individual behavior, family relationships, and impairment of social role functioning (e.g., 7). Operational interpretations of these findings, however, may vary according to the position of the observer and his value orientation. For example, one interpretation in social work stresses the import of "socializing" clients, thereby improving the clients' role functioning.[18] Socialization is implemented by "teaching" the client new behaviors, attitudes, and skills (43, Kamerman in Kahn; 53, pp. 315-316); a very different interpretation stresses change in the client-system, not by teaching but by assuming roles which induce the client-system to change its own rules. The latter is accomplished by requiring the client-system to do what "it" is actually doing and in this way making the

behavior or "symptom" subject to the client's awareness
and subject to change (95). A third interpretation of communication theory focuses on disparity in messages and the
underlying issues which may then be communicated back to
the client-system by the therapist or intervener, e.g., a
confrontation. The latter interpretation, however, is pre-
dicated on respect for the client-systems' frame of reference,
ways of cognitively organizing their experiences, and utilizes
the client-systems' "language of impact" to effect changes
that are "goal-directed and compatible with the clients' viewpoint and self-esteem." Since the latter interpretation draws
upon a systems frame of reference, the intervener-therapist
remains open to new information and to change of his own
system viewpoint (see 26, pp. 404-405).[19]

     Utilizing one approach to communication theory
may lead to an educational role of the therapist-intervener; the client-system may be taught new communication skills or socialized into new behaviors.[20]   Change
in the client-system may also be achieved by "manipu-
lating" the client-system to change its own behavior,
i.e., its communication patterns. For example, the therapist focuses on distortions and contradictions in messages
by means of his confrontation or "release" (see note 19).
Finally, operational interpretations of communication theory
may involve a "prevention" frame of reference leading to environmental correction and institutional change. It is assumed that changes in the "impinging-environment" will
result in positive changes in the client-system: e.g., enhanced communication skills, cognitive development in the
child, improved family and community relationships.

     Theoretical and value distinctions are mirrored in these

different operational interpretations. Socializing, teaching, and educating the client-system may be rejected as forms of social control; confrontation and manipulation may also be rejected as forms of client-system control (and the misuse of influence or power). In other words, communication theory, the process of change and the role of the therapist-intervener may result in varied, compatible and/or opposing operational interpretations and activities.

ISSUES

Before concluding this analysis of trends and shifts in social work's applications of systems theory, two issues, briefly cited above, require clarification and amplification. First is the concept of the hierarchy of systems and second is the concept of model. A basic tenet of general systems theory, the hierarchy of system levels, has been, and is currently, the subject of debate. In a recent publication on social work practice, Meyer rejects this tenet in favor of the "transactional" view proposed and developed by Spiegel. The linear hierarchy is a conceptual handicap because "by focusing at one level, then everything else becomes environment. We focus at points of interaction and neglect those interactions taking place in the extended field over time" (56, p. 127, quoting Spiegel in Grinker). The family case and service delivery systems in the community may be viewed transactionally. "As Spiegel would say, these are all field phenomena; they are not hierarchical or linear, nor do they necessarily derive from each other. They intersect at various points in the existence of all of the factors ... and the balance of forces" (56, p. 128). Thus, Meyer, in accord with Spiegel, views the notion of linear hierarchy of

systems as incompatible with the transactional-field framework.   The rationale given, that is, the dichotomization
between system and environment, may be a misconception
or misuse of general systems theory and the concept of
system hierarchy.   Indeed, system level and system hierarchy are viewed by some theorists as clarifying relations
between systems and increasing communications between
different disciplines--i. e. , multidisciplinary investigations
and collaboration. In any event, the concept cannot be
quickly or easily dismissed.   The very fact that it has
been debated since the middle of the 19th century and is
currently a point of contention suggests that we consider
more fully the underlying issues, their relationships to
scientific developments, and the ways in which these influence and are influenced by the perspectives of the theoretician-practitioner.

The system hierarchy issue is inextricably interwoven with questions concerning the analogistic method,
reductionism, and the use of models.   Bertalanffy notes
that, "Generally speaking, the use of 'analogy' (isomorphism,
logical homology)--or what amounts to nearly the same, the
use of conceptual and material models--is not a half-poetical
play but a potential tool in science" (12, p. 20).   As noted
in the first chapter, Rapoport, like Bertalanffy and other
systems theorists, defends the analogies in general systems
theory as "not mere metaphors.   They are rooted in actual
isomorphisms or homomorphisms between systems or
theories of systems" (70, p. xxi).   The fruitfulness of such
analogies has been illustrated by the notions of feedback and
information (see, for example, Miller quoting Simon, 58,
p. 89).   The idea of hierarchical levels of systems is basic

to the thought of general systems theorists. By disclaiming
this idea one is also disclaiming the search for common,
nontrivial properties among diverse kinds of complex systems
--physical, biological, or social. Bertalanffy quotes Lektorsky and Sadovsky, the Soviet authors reviewing general
systems theory, who "recognize that the kind of isomorphism
with which general systems theory is concerned is a consequence of the fact that in some respects corresponding
abstractions and conceptual models can be applied to different phenomena" (12, p. 20).

Before leaving the question of the analogistic method
and the search for common properties among systems and
moving into questions of reductionism and the organismic
analogy-model, it is appropriate to re-state the meaning of
an hierarchic system and the system-environment issue.

> By a hierarchy I mean a system that is composed
> of interrelated subsystems, each of the latter being,
> in turn, hierarchic in structure until we reach
> some lowest level of elementary subsystem ... it
> is somewhat arbitrary as to where we leave off
> the partitioning, and what subsystems we take as
> elementary [Simon as quoted by Miller in Gray,
> 58, p. 89]. 21

The fact that it is somewhat arbitrary as to what is system
and what is environment, and where we leave off parti-
tioning, is well understood. Nevertheless, both for conceptual and practical purposes we do make these distinctions
and we are aware of the arbitrary selection, just as we are
aware that any hierarchical classification will change over
time (as has been demonstrated in the field of physics) and
will be determined by the position of the observer and his
particular purpose-analysis. Hierarchical system level distinctions are arbitrary, and classifications of system hier-

archy do change.   However, there are criteria for distinguishing system levels--which

> ... are derived from a long scientific tradition of
> empirical observation of the entire gamut of living
> systems ... [and] has led to a consensus that
> there are certain fundamental forms of organiza-
> tion of living matter-energy.   Indeed the classical
> division of subject-matter among the various disci-
> plines of the life or behavioral sciences is im-
> plicitly or explicitly based upon this consensus
> [58, p. 91].

Finally, in light of the criticism that the notion of system
focuses on one level, thereby making "everything else environment" (in contrast to transactional theory which
emphasizes points of intersection in the expanded field), it
is pertinent to cite Watzlawick's statement:

> With the development of the theory of hierarchically
> arranged open subsystems, the system and its en-
> vironment need no longer be artificially isolated
> from one another; they fit meaningfully together
> within the same theoretical framework [95, p. 123]. [22]

Moreover, he points out the usefulness of this conceptual
model (hierarchy) in understanding interactions as part of
the interrelationships among systems.

The organismic analogy applied to psychological and
social system levels has been criticized as reductionistic.
The fact that the notion of organism has been generalized
to the concept of "organized system" (see Rapoport, Bertalanffy, Buckley) and thus may be utilized "to classify various types of systems" (Bertalanffy quoting Lektorsky and
Sadovsky, 12, 20), apparently has not been incorporated
into the thinking of some theorists and practitioners.   This
is reflected in current writings regarding fears of the dangers
of reductionism by organismic analogy.   This writer has

already presented explanations of the generalization of organism and organized system and also the meaning and usefulness of the "organismic analogy" cited by Bertalanffy, Rapoport, Vickers, Haire and others. Bertalanffy in 1962 reaffirmed the fact that "the organismic analogy does not imply 'biologism,' that is, reduction of social to biological concepts, but indicates system principles applying in both fields" (12, p. 30). Furthermore, Bertalanffy, Anatol Rapoport and others emphasize that the system model is a model of only certain aspects of reality (as is every model) and note the danger of any model "when it commits the 'nothing-but' fallacy..." (12, p. 30).

The discussion of general systems theory, and specifically the notions of system hierarchy and organized system, provides a background to consider the "reductionist issue." Comments of several authors may illustrate and give further understanding of its import.

In 1960, Allport, a social psychologist, questioned the validity of the system level concept of general systems theory and stressed the possibility that it would lead to reductionism. It should be understood that Allport's primary investment was in preserving the "integrity" of the personality system and preventing the concept of personality from being dissipated by concepts such as role, interaction, and transaction. Thus, while Allport cites criticism of the "feeble analogizing" that seeks to establish formal identities between system levels, his main thesis is that the "danger in attempting to unify science in this manner lies in the inevitable approach from below, that is, in terms of physical and biological sciences." In this way closed systems or only partly open systems would become our model, "and if we are not careful, human personality in all its fullness is taken a captive into some autistic paradise of methodology" (2, p. 348).

Meyer, a social work writer and educator, recognizes the "attractive possibilities" of systems theory and points out the danger of overvaluing it, thereby making it a closed system (1970). She observes that it may lead to reductionism:

> ... the results of forcing one system of ideas into a mold that would fit another system that is, in fact, unlike it. The danger in this is that neither set of systems maintains its own integrity.... Reductionism could obstruct us from advancing our view of the transactions of the individual in his sphere of society [56, p. 125].

Spiegel, the psychiatric proponent of transactional and social role theory, also expresses concern about reductionism (1971). "Reductionism, in fact, is the sign that aggrandizement of a particular focus is in operation." By over-estimation of one focus (or discipline) other foci are devaluated. Whereas Allport suggested that the physical and biological sciences would overshadow the psychological sciences (and the concept of personality), Spiegel cites the possibility of over-estimating the Psyche focus. The primary danger, according to Spiegel, is the isolation of foci, the failure to see "the interdependence of the foci in the field," and the holding back of multidisciplinary investigation of behavior (87, pp. 59-60).

It may be said, then, that criticisms of reductionism arise out of the theoretician's model and value system and may become a vehicle for supporting the author's particular viewpoint. For example, reductionism can be perceived either as dissipating or over-estimating a "focus" or a system or a discipline. In sum, fears of reductionism are

still evidenced in the 1970's, expressed by different authors,
in different disciplines and contexts, and for different reasons. The significance or utility of these expressions requires continued exploration and assessment. It should be
remembered, however, that the concepts of system level,
isomorphy, and organized system are currently in the
forefront of the thinking and writing of general systems and
information theorists. Buckley (1968) views the notion of
system level as an integral part of open system theory,
and he also employs the concept of isomorphism between
system organization and environmental structure in explicating the development and maintenance of higher-level,
complex, adaptive systems. He reaffirms the generalization of organism to organized system in his writings on
sociocultural systems--"we can speak of society as a system
(in some degree) which, like any of the other levels, comes
to take on certain holistic properties depending on the particular ways the components are bonded or interrelated in
relatively stable ways" (20, p. xxv).

It was noted (in Chap. 1) that at the time Bertalanffy
proposed open system and general systems theory, model-
building was then a popular aspect of the intellectual climate.
Models are still a common subject of debate and a pivot of
criticism in the literature of most fields and disciplines.
One major theme (implied above) is that reductionism leads
to distortions in model-building and model-application. Current writings are replete with references to the inappropriate
application of a model of one aspect of reality to other
aspects of reality. However the organismic analogy often
becomes equated with the organism-organic model which, in
turn, becomes equated with the medical or clinical or disease

model. A model may be condemned when used inappropri-
ately (e. g. , the psychoanalytic model applied to a family or
societal system), or if a particular model is incongruent
with a favored frame of reference. If general systems
theorists seek formal identities between systems, other
theorists concerned with specific disciplines and specific
practice fields seek and stress the differences between
systems and fear that the use of certain models will distort
or destroy the integrity and value of the particular discipline or system level with which they are concerned. While
a particular model, e. g. , the organismic model, may be
rejected on the basis of reductionism, some theoreticians
and many practitioners use a variety of models selectively
and /or in combination, although these models are often of
different levels of abstraction and different aspects of reality.
A particular model may be disclaimed on the basis of reductionism, or because it has become value-laden and its
"status" is modified by shifts occurring in the scientific,
professional, and political arenas.

   General systems theory was and is supported by
some authors because it is psychophysically neutral "without
supposing pathology at the outset" (9; 84, p. 81). Now it
is suggested that general systems theory presents dangers
of reductionism, thus limiting or distorting social work's
perspective and interventive roles. By focusing on one
system or one system level, a transactional view of the
individual-environment is obscured; focusing on the adaptive
model is useful as a means of counteracting the familiar
disease model derived from medicine and psychiatry (56,
pp. 125, 112, 113). Thus social work authors and practitioners seek and employ models of "health" and adaptation

which incorporate various models of systems, environments,
and their relationships.   One such model of system-environment adaptation is the feedback model (based on the notion
of circular causality).   As indicated earlier (see pp. 15-16,
20), Bertalanffy believes the feedback model (and circular
causality) represents a homeostatic, reactive and regressive
model of human behavior rather than the adaptive or "healthy"
model of human behavior.   Whereas Meyer draws upon Menninger's adaptive model because it emphasizes mental health,
not mental illness, Bertalanffy cites Menninger's valuable
description of "mental disease as a series of adjustments
to ever lower homeostatic levels" (16, p. 41).

These brief comments about views and uses of models
are offered simply to illustrate the variations in interpretations and some of the ways these are determined by theo-
retical-value orientations.   A review of the trends in social
work's applications of systems theory provides evidence that
conceptual and practice models are in flux, are being re-
placed, given new emphases and new frames of reference.
Numerous models have been cited in this review of systems
theory: the open system conceptual model contrasted or
combined with the feedback model, the adaptive model
(largely based on ego psychology) contrasted with the disease model (from medicine and psychiatry), the interactional
or transactional models contrasted with the clinical or
psychoanalytic personality models.   References to social
work practice models included: the system information-
processing and feedback model, the crisis theory intervention
model, and the public health and community mental health
models.   Social work practice models are overlapping, not
mutually exclusive.   They all, however, emphasize health

versus pathology (e. g. , adaptive, public health versus organic, disease), current observable behavior versus history and genesis (feedback and circular causality versus clinical and linear cause-effect), larger contexts and models versus narrow, delimited contexts or models (interaction and transaction versus personality as an entity).

In sum, this examination of trends in social work's applications of general systems theory encompassed consideration of the hierarchy of system levels, the use of analogy and isomorphism, the dangers of reductionism, and the utilization of models. The shifts identified in the discussion suggest that general systems theory and its principles and aims are currently perceived and employed in new ways and patterns which are associated with changing theoretical-practice interests and perspectives.

Chapter 3

GENERAL SYSTEMS THEORY AND PSYCHIATRY

INTRODUCTION: BACKGROUND

Although many social workers have repudiated the
psychoanalytic orientation and the medical-disease model,
they continue to draw upon the thinking of current-day
psychiatrists and selectively borrow updated conceptualizations from the psychiatric field. The psychiatric literature,
however, reveals that many psychiatrists themselves are incorporating new concepts and new orientations from the
biological and behavioral and social sciences. In the 1950's
Spiegel wrote about the uses of role concepts in family
therapy and in the doctor-patient relation; Ruesch presented
communication theory as "the social matrix of psychiatry";
Grinker introduced general systems theory to psychiatry in
1956, bringing together the works of information and communication theorists, cyberneticians, biologists, sociologists,
psychologists, anthropologists, philosophers, and political
scientists; Menninger in 1963 (The Vital Balance) blended
psychiatric theory with general systems theory. [23]

Theoretical and practice developments in psychiatry
have had significance for and reverberations in social work.
The following discussion of psychiatric literature only highlights some of the more recent changes and trends in conceptual and practice orientations. [24] The psychiatric writings
selected for consideration here reflect the growing interest

of psychiatry in "larger contexts"--in social systems such
as the family, group, organization, community--and in the
development of theories of psychiatry concerned with inter-
personal-social phenomena rather than intrapsychic or self-
actional personality phenomena. These selected psychiatric
writings contain a fairly wide range and diversity of conceptual and practice notions that differ in varying degrees
from those of traditional psychoanalysis and ego psychology.
Some current psychiatric writers espouse and utilize systems
theory; some use selected systems concepts and demonstrate
their usefulness in family and community interventions;
some combine theories and concepts from different disciplines, e.g., concepts of ego psychology, role, communication, transference; some explicitly oppose selected psychoanalytic notions; and some offer a theoretical framework for
social psychiatry "in tune with" the scientific world of today
and new practice arenas. The writer will attempt to identify
only particular conceptual ideas and practice applications
that have had, or possibly will have, important impact on
social work.

The writings selected for attention will be examined
primarily with respect to general systems theory, other
theories and conceptual notions and the relationship of these
to developments in psychiatric theory and practice. Trends
and issues already identified will reappear, and commonalities
and differences between social work and psychiatry will
emerge.

CURRENT THEORETICAL CONCEPTIONS

Psychiatric theoreticians have contributed to the
development of general systems theory and parallel theories

(e. g. , information-communication theories) since the 1950's.
Many psychiatrists hailed general systems theory as a means
of unifying scientific and discipline theories, and it brought
them into fruitful relations with theoreticians from other
diverse fields. These psychiatrists sought to enlarge their
perspective, bridge gaps in knowledge and communication,
identify convergent trends which would eventuate in a cross-
disciplinary language and stimulate new ways of thinking and
new skills in practice. Psychiatric theory was fertilized by
systems theories, and simultaneously psychiatry expanded
its conceptual tools, practice arenas, and intervention techniques. These "advances," developed or facilitated by general systems theory, emphasize the unification of interdisciplinary theories and practices while simultaneously high-
lighting intradisciplinary incompatibilities. Whereas social
work in the 1960's was concerned with dissolving its method
compartmentalizations and developing a unified theory of
social work practice, psychiatry was concerned with evolving
new theories and practice specializations as well as unifying
the field of psychiatry. [25]

       Current psychiatric writings indicate different posi-
tions taken with respect to the specialization and/or unification of psychiatric theory; for example, some psychiatrists espouse the development of a theory of social psychiatry complementary or in addition to individual-personality
theory (psychoanalytic, ego psychology, growth and self-
actualization theories); some believe that current-day psychiatric problems require the development of a social
psychiatric theory which would displace or replace psychiatric
theories of individual-personality; some focus interest on
specific systems constructs that enhance psychiatric theory

and practice in a variety of fields (e. g., industry, community mental health, psychotherapy, and family therapy);
some explicitly or implicitly revise systems theory concepts
and incorporate them in a new theoretical framework for
psychiatry; and finally, some focus on new "action" developments emerging from the transaction between general
systems theory and psychiatry.   These categories or areas
of interest are overlapping: some are complementary or
compatible, others divisive or incompatible. [26] Stated positions, nevertheless, are sometimes confusing or misleading.
For example, several social psychiatrists, namely Rabkin,
Spiegel, and Jackson, state explicitly that there is no "inherent or necessary incompatibility between these two theoretical approaches" (social psychiatry and psychoanalytic
psychiatry).   The substance of their writings, however,
indicates basic theoretical differences as well as explicit
rejection of psychoanalytic and ego psychology constructs
considered invalid or inappropriate (e. g., 42; 85, p. 353).

      Rabkin rejects concepts of "inner-space," e. g.,
psychic structure, psychic energy, affect, and the "unconscious" mechanism. [27] His analysis of these concepts is
similar in many ways to the analyses of other authors
(representing psychiatric writings from the U. S., Great
Britain, and the Soviet Union).   In fact, he draws heavily
on the ideas of Dewey and Sullivan as well as the thinking
and writings of authors from fields other than psychiatry.
Although there are similarities and commonalities revealed
in these various writings, the basis for rejection of "inner-
space" concepts and the emphasis given to their rejection
and to conceptual substitutions vary.   Rabkin uses somewhat
idiosyncratic terminology; nevertheless, a number of his

ideas appear in current psychiatric literature. Affect and
other "personality" concepts are viewed as occurring in
"outer-space"--they are considered unscientific in their
current form and are re-defined as interpersonal and social
phenomena, e.g., interactions and transactions. Rabkin
asserts that the unconscious is a fundamental Freudian assumption ("supported by certain rhetorical devices"), namely,
that psychoanalytic theory and/or the psychoanalyst is "infallible."
In other words, he claims that the notion of the unconscious
does not allow for the reality of patients' lack of knowledge
or "ignorance," and consequently the "healing powers" of
knowledge and education are overlooked. Thus, he takes
issue with psychoanalytic and ego psychology theorists,
e.g., D. Rapaport and M. Gill, who believe that notions
of conscious and unconscious are valid inferences from
empirical observations. Moreover, Rabkin disallows the
adaptive model, as conceived by these theorists, because it
is based on the duality of the individual-personality and the
"average expectable environment" (69, pp. 40, 41; Ch. 4,
especially pp. 89, 90).

Spiegel, in his recent publication Transactions, conveys acceptance of current psychoanalytic theory which
describes "the process within the individual," and "which
refers to the personality as a system in its own right." He
also employs psychoanalytic concepts, such as unconscious
wishes and fantasies, in his family case analyses. However,
he opposes the notion of personality as an entity--"anything
said to be an entity [e.g., personality] ... has to be spread
around or divided up between various foci in the field. [It]
... would tend to dissolve under transactional inquiry."
Spiegel does not propose the transactional viewpoint as the

sole model of reality; he believes, unlike Grinker, that
descriptions of self-actional, interactional and transactional
processes are required. Nevertheless, he is mainly concerned with investigations of small group phenomena (specifically the family and the doctor-patient relationship) as
the empirical base for developing a social theory of disturbed behavior. Thus, social role and value orientation
are the key concepts in his transactional framework; they
explicate individual behavior problems and family relationship disturbances (87, pp. 35, 42-43, 255).

Jackson, in a similar vein, writes about symptoms,
defenses, and personality as terms that "describe the individual's typical interactions which occur in response to a
particular interpersonal context, rather than as intrapsychic
entities" (42, p. 388). It is apparent that Jackson, Rabkin,
and a number of other social psychiatrists concur that personality is not an entity; it exists only in its social context,
thus it is the social context that must be understood and
"treated." This idea of personality requires a new theoretical framework (not the psychoanalytic or psychothera-
peutic) with new conceptual tools, which in turn involve
different notions of space-time and causality and different
orientations to processes of change and adaptation (42,
p. 390). Finally, Ruesch writes of the "revolutionary
changes in psychiatric theory" and develops a general
systems theory of human behavior based on communication
constructs. He summarizes the changes characteristic
of social psychiatry:

> As we have moved from structure to process,
> from statics to dynamics, from single entities
> to multiple entities, and from univariate to multi-
> variate approaches, we have taken a decisive step

> away from linear thinking and the observation of
> simple phenomenology toward circular or more
> complex thinking and the consideration of more
> general processes. This is about where we now
> stand [78, p. 155].

These brief psychiatric references deal with familiar
themes and issues; however, they are presented from the
stance of the "new" psychiatry with its new perspectives,
definitions, and emphases pertaining to both theoretical and
ideological commitments. They highlight obvious similarities
to current social work writings (see pp. 55-57). The similarity and/or congruence may be due in part to social work's
selective "psychiatric borrowing" and in part to the joint
interests and common problems of the two professions.
Nevertheless, the selectivity of social work's borrowing,
the importation of new concepts and new commitments, are
influenced and modified by social work's heritage--its
"theory," its subculture, and traditional practice patterns.
While social work may appropriately and usefully combine
different concepts (new and old), it may also combine or
simultaneously utilize incompatible theories-constructs, or
draw upon and utilize incompatible conceptual notions for
different situations or purposes. Thus, current emphasis
upon the "here and now," on larger contexts, on social interactions and transactions, does not preclude concurrent
emphasis upon concepts of "inner-space," e.g., psychic
energy, tension discharge, ego defense. This conceptual
approach or pattern may characterize social work knowledge
and skills as well as social work attitudes and beliefs regarding scientific theory, research, and professional practice.

In this context--that is, the relationship between
social work and social psychiatry--it is pertinent to cite

Spiegel's current (1971) assessment of the two disciplines.
In his opinion, social work, like social psychiatry, is an
applied science "in search of a basic science which has not
yet been developed." Unlike social psychiatry, however,
"social work has had to meet the demands of its clients by
elaborating methods based on ad hoc or borrowed concepts,
piecing them together in the best possible working philosophy...." Since there is no social theory of disturbed behavior, "the psychiatric social worker merely conducts a
form of psychotherapy.... Calling this practice casework
obscures the fact that it is based on the same theory of
disturbed behavior as is psychotherapy." Social psychiatry
has not yet faced "its impasse"; it does not exist as a field
of practice (87, pp. 91, 92).

Further examination of current psychiatric writings
pinpoints positions regarding: 1) the "status" of general
systems theory as a theory and method; 2) the notion of
system level hierarchy (involving analogy and isomorphism);
3) the use of models incorporating selected systems concepts; 4) the use of other constructs and theories integrated
in new or modified orientations and frameworks. [28] As
noted, this "sampling" reveals certain similarities and differences with social work writings and also an important
common underlying pivot, namely, the system-environment
configuration. There is basic concern with ways of understanding the person and his social institutions; the system-
environment relationship is thus a recurring persistent
theme.

APPLICATIONS OF GST TO PSYCHIATRIC
THEORY AND PRACTICE

Ecological and Transactional Models

Some general observations and conclusions emerge
from the review of current psychiatric literature related to
or based upon systems theory. [29] "System" (as of 1970)
continues to be an important concept in psychiatric literature
although it appears in new contexts and with some modifications.   The notion of system is placed in broader con-
texts--for example, in an ecological framework or in transactional theory. [30] Systems are ecological systems,
systems in a transactional field, systems in a network.
Ecological and transactional theories or viewpoints indicate fundamental commonalities in concepts and terminology.
These orientations and theories are pinpointed and developed
by social psychiatrists primarily concerned with "action
systems," with operationalizing abstract theory for practice.
They incorporate the system concept and combine selected
aspects of other theories (e.g., field theory, role theory,
communication theory).   Stated differently, ecological and
transactional viewpoints or theories combine and interweave
a number of constructs for operational purposes.   It is not
surprising, therefore, that the proponents of the ecological
and transactional frameworks apply these to therapeutic and
change processes in family and community systems.   Moreover, the ecological and transactional frames of reference
are directed toward and involve interdisciplinary relationships and practice approaches.

In sum, they focus upon the relationships between
systems-in-the-field, the network as a field of connected
points--with lines between the points representing reciprocal

interaction, transactions between individual, family and
society (see, for example, 33, 69, 87). Theorists primarily
focusing on systems (typically the family system) in ecological and transactional frameworks give emphasis to the
intersecting points in a network or field, to the interfaces
between systems rather than systems per se. In other
words, the ecological and transactional frameworks focus on
observable social behaviors, communications at connecting
points in a network and in interface phenomena. These
orientations and constructs: 1) modify and redefine the
notion of individual-personality; 2) interweave the individual
(system) and environment as a whole; 3) reject the linear
hierarchy of general systems theory and system level isomorphisms in favor of the transactional principle of simultaneous reciprocal reverberations in systems in a field. [31]

  Both Rabkin and Jackson claim that the system level
notion and the use of analogy and isomorphisms are not
valid scientific constructs: moreover they are reductionistic
as exemplified in the organismic analogy (69, pp. 141-143).
Rabkin implies that the metaphors and models of individual
psychiatry are transferred from individuals to groups. In
this way, social organisms are conceived as possessing the
same characteristics as the individual. Furthermore the
organismic analogy makes use of the medical-psychiatric
model (and in this way social groups are assigned diagnostic
labels applying to individuals--e. g., the schizophrenic
family). His solution to the inappropriate use of the
organismic analogy and medical model is to develop a
model of social structure that does not dichotomize the
individual-environment, namely, the concept of network and
the interface model (69, pp. 143-148). Jackson shares

Rabkin's concern about "classifying families according to
the presence or absence of individual pathology.... We
must avoid imposing the elements of individual theory onto
the family model. That is, there is no evidence for the
isomorphism of the two theoretical models" (42, p. 389).

While the ecological and transactional approaches (as
depicted by Auerswald, Rabkin, Spiegel, Jackson) reject
linear hierarchy of system levels based on the notion of
isomorphisms and also reject the organismic analogy-model,
they accept and employ open system theory with its concepts of negentropy and principle of equifinality. Notions of
system wholeness, steady state, and boundary are not referred to "as such"; they are recast, not rejected. Rabkin
uses the term "network boundary"--"although networks are
theoretically open-ended and unbounded, they are generally
limited for practical purposes in terms of a specific problem of interest" (69, p. 144). Spiegel writes about "foci
in the field"; the term foci, e. g. , Psyche and Soma, appears,
at times, to be synonymous with the term system(s). For
example, when three systems (Psyche, Group, Society) are
studied, "the system in the middle tends to fade from awareness." While he does not accept the system level and
system hierarchy notions, he discusses the danger of "ob-
literating boundaries between foci" (fusion), the fact that
"we do not know the boundaries or limits of the field, " the
difficulty in determining the "cut-off points between self-
actional, interactional and transactional descriptions" (87,
pp. 40, 66-68, 78).

Auerswald utilizes "the ecological systems model. "
His systems approach and ecological systems model focus
on the "interfaces and communication processes taking place

there" (6, pp. 374-375). He further states that the "ecological systems model, by clarifying and emphasizing the
interfaces between systems, allows for the use of a variety
of theoretical models which have to do with interactional
processes and information exchange" (6, p. 375). Both
Auerswald and Rabkin discuss the utility of crisis theory
within the ecological frame of reference, particularly in that
crisis theory, like communication theory, provides models
which bridge "the conceptual systems of single disciplines"
(6, p. 375). In light of social work's interest in, and application of, crisis theory, [32] Rabkin's interpretation is
pertinent:

> Given a network of interconnected situations, any
> set of circumstances that disrupts what was pre-
> viously going on can be viewed as a crisis; a time
> of opportunity and a time of danger. Any change,
> whether helpful or not, is then a crisis and tends
> to affect all other systems in the network under
> study.... Crisis theory provides a means of
> theoretically coping with the large volume of data
> that inevitably is involved when multiple 'fixes'
> are employed in the analysis of a given problem
> [p. 69, p. 175].

Crisis theory thus may be used in an ecological or
transactional framework; it may also be used as part of
general systems theory with its concept of system level
hierarchy. It is amenable to various theoretical frameworks and it is typically viewed as a valuable tool in understanding and analyzing change process. Duhl, a social-
community psychiatrist, writes about the commonalities
(isomorphisms) of change processes (involving therapeutic
and/or social intervention techniques) at the individual,
family, organization, and community level; he observes that
crisis theory facilitates generalization of the change process

and he also translates crisis theory into system information-
processing concepts (e. g. , input overload or input vacuum,
dissonance of new input with stored information, accommodation to new information resulting in cognitive restructuring
and new patterns of organization) (26, pp. 401-403, 407, 408).

Ecological and transactional frameworks incorporate
selected concepts and processes of information-communication
theory (which may be considered as part of general systems
theory or as a parallel theory). Since both approaches are
operational, are focused upon human beings in their relationships with other persons, concepts of normality-pathology
as well as therapy are explicated in terms of communication
patterns, processes, and skills. Grinker, discussing communication (verbal and nonverbal) in the therapeutic relationship, states:

> Messages are received, acknowledged, and cor-
> rected in a cyclic transaction which changes in
> time and by virtue of the communication feedbacks.
> Hence, learning occurs for both. ... Roles are
> expressed by forms of communication which vary
> with the nature of the current transaction. ...
> Communications within the transactions (expressed
> in forms of role performance) take place in a
> 'field,' an ever changing matrix which affects and
> is altered by the persons involved. 33 In other
> words, the practitioner must recognize that within
> the field a system can be studied only in process
> with another system by the observer who consti-
> tutes a third system [33, pp. 7, 20, 21].

Grinker and Spiegel, thus, draw on field theory as part of
their transactional approach. It should be noted that their
conception of field theory is not the typical Lewinian concept
of field, but is their own idiosyncratic definition. 34 According to Spiegel, " 'field' is a vague, all-purposed word." He
refers to Maxwell's statement in Matter and Motion, namely,

that "a field is a portion of the universe that we make the subject of our investigations," and he then recasts the definition of field as "a transactional statement ... it is the extent of our investigations ... if the field is transactional, then all its parts are interdependent" (87, pp. 39, 40, 41).

It is of particular interest that the proponents of the ecological or transactional frameworks (Rabkin, Auerswald, Jackson, Spiegel, Grinker) are not "behaviorists" nor do they depict their therapeutic strategies and techniques as behavior-modification. While their focus is on behavior as an observable social process (information-communication within interactional and transactional systems), in contrast to personality concepts (e.g., affect, ego defense),[35] they do not view it as "behaviorism." The latter term, according to Rabkin, was formerly employed as "the only alternative to the metaphors of inner-space." In today's social psychiatry it is possible to distinguish between "vulgar behaviorism" and "outer-space" which contains behavior. He points out that Chappell's four refinements of Watsonian behaviorism make it "possible to talk about behavior without using inner-space metaphors or having to accept the crude behaviorism of Watson" (69, pp. 51-52).[36]

Spiegel cites "Narrow 'behaviorism' based on either classical or operational conditioning and ... the 'learning theory' formulations derived from them" as illustrative of the error of "skipping of foci." This type of behaviorism reduces complexity extensively but offers only a limited contribution to transactional inquiry and interdisciplinary research. "What is objectionable is the doctrinal assertion, so often put forth, of the necessity of rigorous exclusion of intervening systems in order to preserve scientific 'purity'

and methodological precision." He also observes that "all
behaviorist theories of learning based on the stimulus-
response model, for example, are self-actional. They are
extremely incomplete" (87, pp. 65, 66, 394n). These statements reveal Spiegel's convergence with the views of
Bertalanffy and other general systems theorists. Indeed,
Spiegel comments:

> Both General Systems Theory and Communications
> Theory have something in common with the trans-
> actional approach which I use. All three approaches
> attempt to frame a way of organizing the data of
> behavior so that they will not be imprisoned by
> the specialized disciplines and yet can be related
> to them for technical purposes. All three try to
> make a place for openness and change, for novelty
> and creativity as well as for sameness and con-
> tinuity over time, within a consistent if not 'unified'
> framework. They differ in the conceptual materials
> and technical resources which they use for the
> organization of the data. At this point in time, it
> cannot be said which approach is more useful or
> valid [87, p. 3 fn. 2].

Particular attention has been given here to the ecological and transactional theories-models currently favored
by a group of social psychiatrists. They represent two
"larger context frameworks" that incorporate and modify
systems constructs (e.g., system level) in conjunction with
other concepts and theories (e.g., field, role, communication). They are appealing to social work in that they are
middle-range, operational, interdisciplinary frameworks
that allow for considerable latitude in practice interventions
and are compatible with social work's humanistic orientation.
Finally, ecological and transactional theories are conceived
as models that bring system-environment into a unified
whole, unlike the organismic-medical model or the adaptive model which are reductionistic and/or dichotomize

system and environment; they redefine notions of personality
and environment (social structure), concepts of normality and
pathology, and present new types of therapeutic strategies
and techniques.

Other Psychiatric Models

Different positions and approaches have been developed
by other psychiatric authors. Some have interrelated general systems theory and psychiatric theory so as to develop
both "generalized" and "specific" theories for the field of
psychiatry. This transaction between general systems
theory and psychiatry is expressed, for example, in Ruesch's
generalized communication theory, Grinker's symbolic system
theory, Schefflen's "psychosomatic" system theory, and also
in the more specific theories such as Arieti's unifying theory
of cognition, Ullman's unifying theory of therapeutic and
community process, and Rizzo's general systems theory
approach to growth and development. [37] These contributions
tend to be more abstract than operational; in various
instances, however, the authors have applied their theories
to specific fields (e.g., industry and community, education,
psychotherapy). Although they relate to different fields or
different system levels, they all have a unifying aim.
General systems theory is typically the basis of, or framework for, the unification.

All the authors of these particular writings[38] accept
and utilize the general systems construct of system level
hierarchy as well as other systems constructs, such as the
notion of negentropy and the principle of equifinality. Moreover, they view general systems theory and the system
model as appropriate for overcoming the duality of individual

and society, soma and psyche, and as useful in unifying
psychiatric theories and therapies. Their interest in a
unified theory or in unifying theoretical linkages is addressed
to psychiatry rather than to interdisciplinary theories. This
unifying approach to psychiatry utilizes the system model to
conceptualize the system-environment relationship and con-
trasts markedly with the ecological and transactional approaches. Also, unlike the ecological and transactional
theories, general systems theory is considered a "well-
formed theoretical framework" and is not employed "metaphorically to describe a way of thinking and an operational
style" (6, p. 374). Finally, whereas these theories and
concepts of GST are aimed at the unification of psychiatry,
the ecological and transactional theories are presented as
replacements, additions, or substitutes for the theories of
individual disciplines. [39]

A considerable number of current psychiatric writings
(more numerous than those cited in this chapter) focus on
systems theory in action. They range widely in their
approaches and applications. [40] All of these "action" applications have a common denominator, namely, the role of
the psychiatrist in change processes. The particular aspect
of systems theory, and the particular system level target,
as well as the scope of the practice problem and the level
of conceptual analysis, vary greatly. A few illustrations of
these variations will suffice. For example, these "action"
articles may apply a particular system concept (e.g., steady
state), the system as a "holistic" concept, or general
systems theory, including its basic concepts and principles,
to the family system, the community system, and/or nation-
al-societal systems. The application of a specific concept

or a theoretical orientation may be utilized in analyzing the
change process in a single family interview, in a series of
family interviews, in a specific community health program,
or in social planning at the national level (e. g., national
planning for community mental health programs and for new
approaches in law enforcement and the administration of
justice). In a study of "steady state," interaction process
analysis was applied to the empirical data of a single interview situation (see 23). It was possible (in this research
study) to trace steady state disturbances, regulator activity,
and change. In other words, steady state was a "divining
rod" to identify change and to determine the effectiveness of
a therapeutic practice-technique.

Other authors who write about systems theory and
family therapy utilize clinical material to support a particular theory or concept. It may be recalled that Jackson, a
family theoretician and practitioner, espouses the interactional perspective. His paper, "The Individual and the
Larger Contexts," does not focus on empirical data per se
but provides a paradigm of marital interaction. The latter
illustrates his thesis that the family may be "viewed as a
mutual causative system, whose complementary communication reinforces the nature of their interaction. The therapist can look for rules that govern this system; therapy
then consists of the therapist behaving in such a way that
the rules must change" (42, p. 392). Another author,
writing about family therapy, utilizes a still broader theoretical perspective, applying general systems theory to the
human life cycle. Family therapy is analyzed in light of
these abstract theoretical concepts and propositions and
then "operationalized" in a specific case. Brief excerpts

of the therapeutic communications illustrate the way in which
meaningful dialogues among family members can be achieved
(64, p. 447).   Finally, a paper which applies general systems theory to multiple family therapy incorporates numerous concepts and principles from information and communication theory, small group theory, field theory, general
systems theory, including concepts of system levels, hierarchy, goal seeking, and isomorphisms among non-living
and living systems--all of which may ultimately create "a
true universality of knowledge..." (47, p. 431). [41]

As noted, some authors apply general systems theory
in their analyses of community action programs and social
planning.   One approach is to focus on a particular community mental health program--e.g., the way systems theory
was employed in creating a service delivery program in
the community.   Hansell concludes his discussion of a particular community service program with the statement that:
"The formulation of a mental health service network as a
system is an acknowledgment of the related facts that the
human personality is a system, that society can be understood as a system, and that the casualty management network is a subsystem of that society" (38, p. 370).   A
second approach is to evaluate the effectiveness of and locate
the deficiencies in community service delivery programs
(86).   A third approach is to demonstrate the way in which
systems analysis and ecological models facilitate the social
planning process (27).   A fourth approach employs the system model to generalize the change process, "so that the
individual therapist will see the analogues of his work with
individuals, in work with families or organizations and the
communities ... the concept of parallels or isomorphic

qualities in each level of systems is part of the [general systems] theory" (26, p. 407). A fifth approach explicates the new role of psychiatry in the community which demands "a generic system of psychiatry" with a multi-level approach that includes, but goes beyond, "intrapsychic pathology." Rome's paper discusses the relationship of psychiatry and social change; psychiatry and psychiatric institutions are reshaped by changes in the eco-political systems and require the development and utilization of "a psychiatric information system [which] can extend its scope" into community planning and decision-making (76, Ch. 16, p. 332).

All of these psychiatric writings--whether focused on the family, group, organization, community, national system level and/or whether guided by a particular concept, proposition, aspect, or interpretation of general systems theory--incorporate and emphasize: social-environment contexts such as ecological models, networks of systems, systems in a field, as well as the interfaces between systems; the utility of information-communication theory; the importance of cross-disciplinary fertilization and "the orchestration of intra- and inter-disciplinary cooperation" in order to understand the complex phenomenon of man (76, p. 323). Finally, in all of these articles and papers there is evidence of pervasive concern with conceptual models and tools with which to look at man and his institutions and "foment the change of adaptation" (76, p. 323).

Themes and dilemmas delineated in the discussion of general systems theory trends and applications in social work and psychiatry included: the nature and definition of personality and environment, the duality of psyche-soma, individual-society, system-environment; the nature and

meaning of causality, especially as this bears upon the
relationship between system and environment and the processes of change and adaptation; the validity and utility of
systems constructs, e.g., structure, function, and process,
and system level hierarchy; the compatibility of the machine
model and models of man-in-his-ecological-relationships;
the compatibility of theories of individual personality and
society (environment); the nature of interdisciplinary theories
and practices; the relationship of discipline theories to
abstract, generalized theories, and the relationship of discipline and abstract theories to the development of a unified
theory of human behavior. These theoretical concerns have
been with us in the past; they beset us anew in the context
of the current scientific, economic, political, and social
scene. The following section of the book does not provide
answers or solutions to the questions and issues that
have emerged; however, it presents several perspectives
that may yield some new insights for the human professions,
including social work. The writer's interests and biases
are evident: 1) in the selection of materials and the messages they convey; 2) in the emphasis upon scientific-
theoretical developments that may well have long-range
implications for practice.

NOTES FOR PART II

1. See, for example, writings of Carlson, Gordon, Hearn,
    Hollis, Lathrope, Meyer, Polsky, Shafer, Shul-
    man, Sister Mary Paul Janchill, Stein.

2. This refers to the notion of models. Numerous
    articles have explicated the concept of model and
    have differentiated between analytic, conceptual or
    master models and concrete, empirical or "work-
    ing" models.

The practitioner utilizes a conceptual or analytic model as he constructs the working model of the concrete problem-situation. He sees where the congruities and discrepancies occur between the conceptual model of the system and the actual event. 'He becomes ... the observer, analyzer, and modifier of the conceptual model he is using' [89, p. 156; and Stein quoting Chin, 24, p. 201].

Lathrope quotes Erikson, who writes that the practitioner "must maintain a constant inner traffic between his often dramatic observations and his conceptual models however crude" (48, p. 49).

3. See for example, Ch. 3 in Part II, which focuses on systems theory and psychiatry, and Ch. 5 in Part III, which focuses on concepts and semantics.

4. Specific references are found in Chin's intersystem model which focuses upon the connectives, both conjunctive and disjunctive, between the client and the helping systems (24, p. 208). Polsky uses a social system model to explicate the role of the helping system in mediating between the client system and family-work systems and the import of change in the helping system as the client-system changes (68). Erikson deals with the "transactions taking place between deviant persons on the one side and agencies of control on the other," i.e., "boundary-maintaining mechanisms" (49, p. 10, Kai T. Erikson as quoted by Lathrope).

5. See, for example, references: 22, 25, 46, 48, 49, 50, 66, 68, 79.

6. Proposed master models of social work include notions of social work as an action intersystem, the nature of human organizations (especially the system-environment complex), the nature of social work, its locus and focus, its change strategies and interventions (39, pp. 63-70).

7. See the earlier discussion of system classifications-- e.g., analytic or conceptual, empirical or concrete, and also Lathrope's discussion of master models and working models (48). See also Meadows,

et al., defining the relationship between theory, model, and the empirical world (54).

8. The "matching" of system-environment, as presented by Gordon, involves the distribution of entropy and also the information-processing occurring in the transaction (action intersystem) (30).

9. Sister Mary Paul Janchill, in her article on "Systems Concepts in Casework Theory and Practice," published in 1969, explains that negative entropy of open systems occurs "by importing more energy from its environment than it spends" (84, p. 80). Whereas, open systems do indeed import energy as well as information, open systems are enabled to develop towards greater complexity and differentiation largely on the basis of importation, processing, etc., of information as well as energy. (See Ch. 1 with regard to the Second Industrial Revolution and the transformation of information.)

10. In the earlier discussion of systems theory it was stated that all systems (at different levels) could be analyzed with respect to the concepts of structure, function and history. For example, system structure is evident at the biological, personality, family, group, and community-society levels of systems. (As suggested, the notion of "structure" has become in itself a pivot of debate--both conceptually and terminologically.)

11. Ego has been defined as the "homeostatic device for finding balance between the demands of the individual and the requirements of reality" (Verbal communication from Sheila B. Kamerman, see chapter by Sheila Kamerman, et al.--in 43, Kahn, in press). It is well known that ego psychology has expanded and modified the concept of ego and ego defenses. The origins of the ego, the primary autonomous functions of the ego, and the ego's functions of coping are included in ego psychology theory. Social work has made use of these concepts, some of which are translated into systems terms. For example, ego coping and mastery functions are considered consonant with open system concepts of negentropy and equifinality (See Kamerman in 43). Gordon states that coping patterns of the personality

system need to be "matched" with "the 'qualities
of the impinging' environment..." (30, p. 10).

12.   This is currently reflected in the utilization of pre-
      ferred practice models--adaptive, public health,
      crisis, and developmental--in contrast to the
      clinical, medical, or "disease" model. The cy-
      bernetic model (e. g., the notion of feedback and
      deviation-amplifying and deviation-counteracting
      processes) is also a currently favored approach
      to short-term psychotherapy and structured be-
      havior change (see for example 66).

13.   Articles on crisis intervention with groups (see 91)
      emphasize these factors as well as the therapeutic
      effectiveness (as judged by crisis outcome criteria).

14.   Rabkin discusses the "recent demand for social psy-
      chiatric services that both reach to a broad cross-
      section of the population and are conducted within
      a brief time interval. " He also quotes Bellak
      regarding the danger of "a reversion to the pre-
      analytic days of the common sense approach, the
      purely humane approach, which will involve the
      loss of the valuable hypotheses that Freud applied"
      (69, p. 181; 8, p. 4).

15.   Systems theory would expand this to include the
      "matching" of the individual or family system with
      the impinging environment (See 30).

16.   This brief statement regarding the public health model
      and its preventive intervention strategies is quite
      different from the description of crisis theory and
      intervention; for example, tension discharge and
      mastery, cognitive clarification and restructuring
      are concepts largely drawn from ego psychology.

17.   Watzlawick cites three dimensions of communication
      theory: syntactics, semantics, and pragmatics.
      The latter provides some basic conceptual tools
      for family therapy. While pragmatics of com-
      munication emphasizes the behavioral effects of
      communication (normal and abnormal) it includes,
      to some extent, syntactics (the transmission of
      information) and semantics (the meaning of in-
      formation) and its frame of reference is inter-

actional; it is the interaction system that focuses
upon the observable manifestations of relationships
(95).

18. Socialization, as utilized in anthropology or sociology,
    is viewed as a "scientific" (value-free) concep-
    tualization of the process whereby an individual
    (usually a child) incorporates the "expected" be-
    haviors and roles of his social-cultural system.
    On the other hand, it may be viewed as a "value-
    laden" concept which supports and/or reinforces
    the status-quo of the larger social system and con-
    trols deviance from traditional rules and norms.

19. These comments have reference primarily to social
    work literature, although the brief quote from
    Duhl anticipates subsequent discussion of psychiatric
    literature--with reference to the application and
    utilization of systems theory. Duhl employs the
    notion of system levels in his analysis of the pro-
    cess of change, intervention and therapy. Rabkin,
    also a social psychiatrist, draws upon communi-
    cation theory and emphasizes its usefulness in
    developing a theory of social psychiatry. The
    family therapist focuses upon the nature and mean-
    ing of the family's communications as they define
    and control family relationships. Although at times
    Rabkin appears to support the "teaching" or educa-
    tional role of the therapist, his approach is not to
    "teach communication skills" to families nor to
    give advice and guidance. Rather he utilizes a
    technique called "release," which he explains as
    both a social process and a behavioristic concept.
    When the therapist understands the underlying com-
    munication problems in the family he deals with
    these problems by the use of release. The latter
    may involve giving a task to a family member in
    order to release the family members from a repeti-
    tive pattern or rule that prescribes and limits
    spontaneous, "healthy" family relationships (69,
    pp. 52-58).

20. The implicit or explicit goal may be the client's adjust-
    ment to his larger social system or the client's
    self-development and personal growth.

21. Miller, perhaps anticipating criticisms of the notion of

hierarchy, states that, "It would be convenient
for theorists if the hierarchical levels of living
systems fitted neatly into each other like Chinese
boxes. The facts are more complicated, as my
discussion of subsystems and components indicates"
(58, p. 91). This writer finds Miller's explanation of subsystem process and structural component
of considerable interest, especially as it relates
to organization theory and role concepts. Subsequent references to current psychiatric writings
are pertinent to the "hierarchy issue."

22. Watzlawick also quotes Arthur Koestler (The Act of
Creation, New York: The Macmillan Co., 1964),
"Thus the functional units on every level of the
hierarchy are double-faced as it were: they act
as whole when facing downwards, as parts when
facing upwards" (95, p. 123).

23. Like Bertalanffy, Menninger presents psychopathology
in systems terms such as de-differentiation or disorganization, and also like Bertalanffy, he goes
beyond the principle of homeostasis and emphasizes the progressive differentiation and specialization characteristic of complex adaptive higher-
level systems.

24. The writer is not unaware that the "traditional" psychoanalytic and ego psychology theories continue to be
represented in current psychiatric literature and
practice and also continue as a major influence in
social work thinking and activity.

25. There is ample evidence that some social and psychoanalytic psychiatrists view general systems theory
as the basis for a "new" theory of human behavior.

26. It is of some interest to the writer that theoreticians
and practitioners of social psychiatry view themselves both as "future-planners" (social policy
and social legislation) and as "psychotherapists"
of the community as a whole. Indeed, at times
these two perspectives or role dimensions are
equated with each other. (See, for example, Duhl
and Spiegel in Gray, 27, 86).

27. These notions (i.e., concepts of "inner-space") will be

considered further in the following section of the
book (Part III).

28. See earlier statements about psychiatric views and
uses of general systems theory (pp. 58-61).

29. The "sampling" includes thirty psychiatric articles
and papers in addition to five books.

30. See the earlier reference to Meyer's use of Spiegel's
(and Grinker's) transactional theory for social
work practice.

31. The notion of simultaneous reciprocal reverberations
occurring in systems and among systems is basic
to transactional theory. It was noted by Grinker
as the transactional principle (Toward A Unified
Theory of Behavior, 1956) and further developed
and utilized by Spiegel and Grinker in subsequent
writings.

32. See the earlier discussion of crisis theory intervention
and short-term treatment (pp. 39-46). Also,
note Meyer's statement that "crisis theory is by
definition a transactional theory..." (56, p. 180;
43).

33. Grinker substitutes field theory for the system level
hierarchy concept of general systems theory. He,
too, like Rabkin, Jackson, Allport, etc., cites
the danger of reductionism in system level hierarchy and also the danger of extensionism (extend
a biological concept directly to psychology).

> According to field theory ... each organization
> is in process with its environment and with
> other organizations.... Within this field are
> systems (soma, psyche, society, culture, etc.)
> with a varying degree of stability or integration,
> and each with a structure in space and a func-
> tion in time [33, p. 6].

34. See Piaget's discussion of Lewinian field theory in
Structuralism, briefly cited here in note 39, Part
III.

35. Jackson states that, "Adopting the premise of the family

as a system requires us to attend only to present
(observable) process, that is, to ecology rather
than genesis" (42, p. 390, emphasis his). He
discusses the circular or feedback model of
causality and also the deviation-amplifying mutual
causal process and concludes that it is impossible
and irrelevant to distinguish between cause and
its effect. "Only the study of the family as a
contemporary, ongoing system with circular networks of interaction can avoid this pointless and
irresolvable debate" (42, p. 392).

36. See the reference to Rabkin's treatment technique of
"release" as a social process--which differs from
the so-called behavior therapies usually based on
conditioning and learning theory (69, pp. 52, 55,
56).

37. These papers and articles are included in General
Systems Theory and Psychiatry, edited by William
Gray, et al. (31). Some of these chapters are
reprints of articles published in journals, some
are reprints of papers presented at psychiatric
meetings, and some are written specifically for
this book. The majority of the papers were
written in 1966 and 1967.

38. Grinker, in his paper (December, 1966) on "Symbolism and General Systems Theory" (34), applies
the topological theory of psychoanalysis (unconscious,
preconscious, and conscious) and transactional
theory to symbolism. He integrates the transactional concept in systems theory (using Bertalanffy's
formulations) and states that, "General systems
theory includes in its global concepts isomorphism
from cell to society." He also quotes Elasser,
"organisms are semiautonomous, dynamic systems
characterized by hierarchies of order and a high
degree of individuality and with incredible variations" (34, p. 139). His combination of systems
theory and transactional theory with tacit acceptance
of notions of system level and isomorphism is note-
worthy particularly in light of his explicit rejection
of linear hierarchy in transactional theory. See
Part I, Chapter I and Part IV in his book, Psychiatric Social Work: A Transactional Case Book,
published in 1961 (33). See also the above discussion

of ecological and transactional theories.

39.   Auerswald and Rabkin hold that the current interdisci-
      plinary approach is unsatisfactory because it

> ... maintains the vantage point of each con-
> tributor within his own discipline.   While it
> [the interdisciplinary approach] has expanded
> the boundaries of the theoretical framework of
> each discipline to include concepts borrowed
> from other disciplines, only those concepts
> which pose no serious challenge or language
> difficulties are welcomed.   More importantly, I
> think, the interfaces between the conceptual
> frameworks of different disciplines are ignored,
> and, as a result, the interfaces between the
> various arenas of systematic life operation (e.g.,
> biological, psychological, social or individual,
> family, community) represented by different
> disciplines are also ignored [6, pp. 374-375].

The writer cites this quotation for comparison with
current social work literature which stresses the
utility of systems and transactional theories to
"broaden the boundaries" of the case and of social
workers' theoretical perspective.

40.   The ecological and transactional frameworks may be
      placed in this category, i.e., although general
      systems theory is modified, it is applied opera-
      tionally--in "action."

41.   Laqueur also considers the issue of cybernetic models
      and/or models of living systems and models of
      man.   He attempts to demonstrate the usefulness
      of nonliving and living models while accepting the
      differences between them and the dilemma of
      automation versus humanization.

PART III

THE CHANGING FACES OF THEORY:
NEW AND OLD, CONCEPTS AND SEMANTICS

The importance and relevance of theories and models for professional disciplines--specifically social work--is a central thesis of the book. This section pursues the subject of "theory" within an arbitrarily delimited framework and with a particular focus of interest.

The foregoing discussions gave evidence of varying conceptual orientations and the interplay between theory and practice. In this section, the spotlight is on reformulations and revisions of theory; these are illuminated by several selected illustrations of theory-building that combine the old and the new--not as "compromises" nor as "eclectics" but as thorough-going theoretical analyses, evaluations, and syntheses that yield new or updated theories.

87

Chapter 4

APPLICATIONS OF SYSTEMS THEORY
AND STRUCTURALIST THEORY

INTRODUCTION: BACKGROUND

The works of three authors demonstrate significant efforts in theory synthesis and revision. Each author explicates the nature of and rationale for his theoretical review and reformulation. The authors have an impressive command of current scientific developments; these are woven into their particular theoretical perspectives and enable them to modify, rework or reinforce their formulations.

The theoretical orientations and developments of the authors discussed in this section display remarkable similarities. Despite the fact that they are working with distinctly different theories, fundamental commonalities are noted in their reformulations. First and foremost is their utilization of and emphasis on evolutionary theory, biological theory (including embryology, genetics, ethology), and systems theory (especially information-processing theory); each author, with his particular theoretical stance (and each working in a different country), draws upon many identical source materials. Second is the emergence of their theoretical revisions following careful scrutiny of past and current conceptual notions tested in the light of advances in modern biological-physical sciences and in the light of the specific nature and aims of their theoretical revisions; that is, each author arrives at his theoretical developments and

"updatings" through comprehensive, intensive study incorporating the comparative analysis of an extraordinarily wide
range of writings and cross-disciplinary research findings.
Third are their unique and innovative theoretical contributions, which take into account all relevant historical, scientific, and ideological contributions and positions. Finally,
the theoretical perspectives and revisions of these authors
have particular import in that their formulations encompass
conceptual orientations, models, and issues that were explicated in the earlier sections of this book; for example, the
system-environment relationship--wholeness versus duality
or dichotomy; the machine or nonliving versus the living
or human model; the acceptance or rejection of system level
hierarchy; the definition and utilization of concepts of structure, function and process; the varying interpretations of the
construct of causality; the nature of processes of change and
adaptation (normality and pathology); the validity of cross-
system isomorphisms and generalizations; the use of analogy
(e. g., the organismic analogy), and the danger of reductionism.

The following discussion thus attempts to present the
theoretical approaches and/or revisions of three authors
from different fields with different perspectives and aims;
attention is given to the key aspects of their unique and innovative contributions, the ways in which they compare
with (oppose, modify, or extend) the conceptual formulations
and issues delineated in the analysis of trends in general
systems theory and its applications.[1] This examination,
however, will pinpoint considerations of language, terminology, and semantics;[2] indeed, these are explicated by the
authors themselves and have particular value for theoreticians as well as practitioners.

PSYCHOANALYTIC, INSTINCT
AND STRUCTURALIST THEORIES

The authors and publications examined here are:
John Bowlby's recent book, Attachment (Volume I of Attachment and Loss), 1969; Emanuel Peterfreund's (in collaboration with Jacob Schwartz) monograph, Information, Systems,
and Psychoanalysis: An Evolutionary Biological Approach to
Psychoanalytic Theory, 1971; and Jean Piaget's most recent
publication (translated into English), Structuralism, 1970.
Bowlby, a British psychiatrist, is well known for his research on maternal deprivation. The current work on
Attachment is not simply an extension of his observational
studies of the separation of young children from their mothers
providing additional findings relevant to the development of
personality and subsequent psychopathology. This volume
goes much further in that it develops a new type of instinct
theory. [3] Bowlby explains that his model of instinctive behavior is

> ... imported from neighboring disciplines and ...
> is a reflection of the scientific climate of the
> times. It derives partly from ethology and partly
> from behavioural models developed by control
> theory--i. e., control systems with their central
> concepts of information, negative feedback, and
> a behavioural form of homeostasis [18, pp. 17, 18].

Peterfreund, an American psychoanalyst, on the basis of his
many years of practice and study, focuses on "the task of
casting psychoanalytic metapsychology in a form that is more
consonant with contemporary scientific thought..." (65, p. 2
in the Preface, by B. Rubenstein). Through his "interest in
the general problem of biological organization and biological
order, and in information and systems concepts [he began]

to develop an explanatory model for the psychoanalytic process." Peterfreund explains that "this approach provided
[him] with basic concepts and new models around which [he
could organize] an alternative theory for the general body of
psychoanalytic clinical data" (65, p. 11).

The theoretical formulations of Bowlby and Peterfreund are almost identical. Bowlby's work is based on
empirical, observational data of prospective-type research
and is primarily directed toward a revision of instinct theory,
and Peterfreund's work is based on empirical, clinical data
of retrospective-type study and is primarily directed toward
a revision of psychoanalytic theory. Nevertheless, they
revised these respective theories in terms of information-
processing concepts; both Bowlby and Peterfreund explicitly
employ the control system model within an evolutionary biological frame of reference. Instinct theory and psychoanalytic theory are closely intertwined--they both concern human
development, "normal" and pathological. However, instinct
theory is a broad, abstract theory which provides conceptual
tools for various disciplines, including biology, psychology,
psychiatry, sociology, and so forth; psychoanalytic theory,
incorporating aspects of instinct theory, provides a conceptual
model of personality development (normal and pathological)
which is the basis for the conceptualization of the psychoanalytic process. Despite the fact that Bowlby and Peterfreund were working with different kinds of empirical data,
had different "starting points" and goals, their theoretical
reformulations discarded identical traditional conceptual models
and tools and substituted identical new models and tools. It
is of interest that, working independently, [4] Bowlby and Peterfreund explicate the same purpose, namely, to link instinct

theory and psychoanalytic theory to "the main corpus of
present-day biology" and to integrate these theories with
"present-day science" (18, p. 20; 65, pp. 14-15).

Piaget, a Swiss psychologist, has made major contributions to the theory of cognitive development. His
unique experimental research with children provides the
basis for systematic study of cognitive processes; innumerable subsequent studies have been stimulated by Piaget's
original findings and conceptualizations. Although most of
his previous writings primarily focus on the nature and development of intelligence, Piaget has always related his
thinking (e. g., the origins of intelligence) to the relationships between mind and biological organization. In Structuralism, however, he does not deal with empirical data as
such, nor present any one of his specific researches on
cognition. Instead, he presents the notion of structuralism
as an important, basic method of science employed in diverse
disciplines, such as mathematics, physics, biology, psychology, linguistics, sociology, anthropology, and philosophy.
Moreover, he offers an analysis and critique of the principal
structuralist positions in these various fields.

It might appear, initially, that Piaget's Structuralism
has little relevance to systems theory and little in common with
Peterfreund's revision of psychoanalytic theory and Bowlby's
revision of instinct theory. In the first place, there is a
closer affiliation between instinct and psychoanalytic theory
than between these theories and structuralist theories; in
the second place, both Bowlby and Peterfreund explicitly
utilize the information-processing, control system model and
concepts, thereby facilitating comparative analysis; in the
third place, both Peterfreund and Bowlby write from a

psychiatric stance with which social workers are more likely to be familiar--in contrast to Piaget's analysis and recasting of structuralist positions related to his attempt to generalize the epistemology of human intelligence. Nevertheless, even a superficial examination of Piaget's work reveals its relevance to general systems theory and theory-building, as well as its marvelous scope, its originality, and its profound significance.

CONCEPTUAL COMMONALITIES

Structuralist Model and Control Systems Model

The "commonalities" of Piaget's structural theory and the theoretical model (control systems) used by Bowlby and Peterfreund are relevant and meaningful. First, although Piaget does not explicitly employ the information-processing control system model, it is implicit in his conceptualization of structuralism. For example, Piaget defines structures as self-regulating transformational systems, he conceives his theory as "cybernetic structuralism," and he incorporates the notion of feedback and feedback loops in connection with system-environment relationship: "transformation laws ... depend upon the interplay of anticipation and correction ... the range of application of feedback mechanisms is enormous," operational systems are "perfect regulations from a cybernetic point of view," and so forth (67, pp. 15-16). Second, Piaget's Structuralism is inextricably interwoven with and oriented to evolutionary and biological theory. For example, he explains the way in which structures as self-regulating systems are important for evolutionary theory.

Third, Piaget makes explicit his interdisciplinary
view not only of structuralism but of all scientific theories.
Closely connected to Piaget's interdisciplinary approach are
his analysis and revision of structuralist theories in the
light of advances in modern human sciences. Although their
theoretical stances differ, Piaget, Bowlby and Peterfreund
all draw upon modern biological theories, especially ethology
and genetics, anthropology, psychology, and of course, information and cybernetic theories. Recalling statements of
Bowlby and Peterfreund with regard to the connection of
psychoanalytic and instinct theory to twentieth-century scientific theory, it is of interest to note Piaget's statement that
current scientific psychology "is resolutely severed from its
roots in biology" (67, p. 131). Finally, with regard to the
interdisciplinary orientation and the convergence of theories
in diverse fields, Piaget emphasizes that

> ... the fundamental trait of the sciences today is
> the multiplicity of their interactions, which tend to
> form a system closed upon itself with many cross-
> linkings ... thermodynamics with information
> theory, psychology with ethology and biology,
> psycholinguistics with generative grammar, logic
> with psychogenetics and so on ... epistemology
> is in fact increasingly internal to the several
> sciences, dependent upon their cyclic arrange-
> ment, subject to shifts as interdisciplinary rela-
> tions become modified [67, p. 133].

Fourth, Piaget, in the context of structuralism, just
as Bowlby and Peterfreund in the context of the information-
processing control systems model applicable to psychoanalytic
and instinct theories, incorporates the notion of system
levels and hierarchy, the concepts of structure, function,
and history and the ways in which these are interrelated,
the concepts of change and adaptation and the ways in which

these are related to notions of causality. Fifth, as implicitly suggested above, Piaget, Bowlby, and Peterfreund,
in reviewing and revising theories, discuss scientific laws
and levels of explanation, for example, laws governing the
formation of structures. [5] Moreover, discussions of scientific laws or explanations and frames of reference include
considerations of the use of language and problems of terminology and semantics.

Sensori-Motor Theory and Systems Theory

There is another aspect of the commonalities or
similarities between the works of Bowlby, Peterfreund and
Piaget. This does not involve Piaget's Structuralism. It
does, however, highlight the fact that both Bowlby and
Peterfreund utilize and emphasize Piaget's sensori-motor
theory in their revisions of instinct and psychoanalytic
theories--both of which are based upon an information-
processing control systems model. Put differently, both
Bowlby and Peterfreund view Piaget's sensori-motor theory
as compatible with and supportive of their systems model;
both interweave concepts of Piaget's sensori-motor theory
into their revisions of instinct and psychoanalytic theories.
Bowlby comments upon specific experiments and researches
of Piaget in explicating: an "alternative model" of instinctive behavior; the ontogeny of instinctive behavior; a control
systems approach to attachment behavior; the ontogeny of
human attachment and specifically the beginnings of attachment behavior (e.g., the infant's responses to people and the
importance of the mother-figure for sensori-motor development); developments in the organization of attachment behavior (e.g., the way in which more sophisticated elements of attachment behavior are organized as plans with

set-goals, and the handicap of egocentrism in developments
in the organization of attachment behavior). Most of Bowlby's
references to Piaget's experiments indicate that the latter
were replicated in more recent studies (in various countries)
and that Piaget's early findings have been supported. Moreover, Piaget's research findings are easily incorporated
into Bowlby's presentation of attachment behavior in the
context of his control systems model; in other words,
Piaget's conceptualization of "stages" of sensori-motor
development may be understood as one aspect of the development of behavioral systems--from simple to complex, from
S-R or trial-error behavior to goal-corrected behavior and
behavior organized as plans with set-goals (an information-
processing systems approach to behavioral development). [6]
Bowlby also cites Piaget's works in his presentation of "An
Alternative Model" (of instinctive behavior). He states that
"man's capacity to build up a detailed representation of the
world in which he lives--a topic to which Piaget has devoted
a lifetime's work--is obviously far greater than that of
other species" (18, p. 49).

Peterfreund, like Bowlby, incorporates Piaget's
conceptualization of developmental steps which reveal increasingly complex thought processes. Just as Bowlby
refers to Piaget in support of his control systems model
of the development of behavioral systems, so Peterfreund
refers to Piaget in his proposal of an information-processing
systems approach to psychoanalytic theory. Thus, he draws
on Piaget in questioning the validity and usefulness of the
concepts of primary and secondary processes (basic to traditional psychoanalytic theory); he points out that these concepts have little relevance to contemporary scientific thought

and, unlike Piaget's sensori-motor theory, are of little help
in conceptualizing developmental steps. Peterfreund, however, does not utilize Piaget's research findings alone to
support his theory revision. He devotes a whole chapter
to the sensori-motor theory of Piaget, taking note of "Piaget's
deeply evolutionary, biological approach" (65, p. 365).[7]

Peterfreund demonstrates specific conceptual similarities between Piaget's sensori-motor theory and the information-systems frame of reference. He suggests that
the concept of aliment is closely related to the concept of
information; the concept of schemata is closely related to
the concept of structure (i. e., existing information-processing
programs), the concept of accommodation is equated with
the notion of reprogramming existing programs on the basis
of new information input (65, p. 366).[8] Although it is possible to translate Piaget's sensori-motor concepts into information systems terms, Peterfreund recognizes that this
is not an optimum approach; he therefore reconceptualizes
the empirical generalizations of the six stages of sensori-
motor development in terms of systems theory. Finally,
Peterfreund points to the value of uniting Piaget's data and
generalizations with those of the psychoanalytic information-
systems model; he emphasizes and illustrates the way the
interests of Piaget and psychoanalysis coincide. His concluding comment is essentially the same as Bowlby's statement quoted above (see p. 96), namely, the multiple ways in
which man organizes the world about him--which can then
be conceptualized in an information-control systems frame of
reference.[9] In sum, the conceptual similarities between
Piaget's sensori-motor theory and systems theory are explicated by both Peterfreund and Bowlby.[10]

STRUCTURALIST THEORY AND GENERAL
SYSTEMS THEORY: IMPLICATIONS

The relationship between Piaget's structuralist theory
and general systems theory (briefly discussed above) has
implications that deserve further attention. Piaget's structuralism is relevant to the theoretical purview of social
work and may suggest new or additional conceptual horizons
and new ways of thinking. The first, and perhaps most
apparent, similarity between structuralist and systems
theories is their high level of abstraction and the breadth
of scope. Neither, therefore, is "operational" but both have
significance with respect to practical applications. Second,
they are both interdisciplinary and serve as conceptual links
among various disciplines and diverse fields. Third, both
theories search for and identify the commonalities of structures and systems "wherever they may be found." In other
words, both theories seek to identify those aspects that are
common to all varieties of structures and all varieties of
systems.

Fourth, Piaget points out that the notion of structuralism is not a new one; structuralism, like systems
theory, has a "long history, which forms part of the history
of the sciences, even if in comparison with the hypothetical-
deductive method it is of comparatively recent origin" (67,
p. 136). The fact that Piaget defines structuralism as a
method and not a "doctrine," implies that it must meet all
the criteria of a scientific method. General systems theory
is also viewed as a scientific method--which, according to
critics, requires further development (i. e., rules to establish
and to apply systems principles). Piaget's position regarding structuralism is very much like that stated by systems

theorists such as Bertalanffy and Rapoport; he writes that

> ... the most important conclusion to be distilled
> from our series of investigations is that the study
> of structure cannot be exclusive and it does not
> suppress, especially in the human sciences and in
> biology, other dimensions of investigation. Quite
> the contrary, it tends to integrate them, and does
> so in the way in which all integration in scientific
> thought comes about, by making for reciprocity
> and interaction [67, p. 137]. [11]

It would appear, then, that both the structuralist and the
systems approach when applied to the study of man can be
understood "as an effort to restore meaning ... while ad-
hering to the principles of disciplined generalizations and
rigorous deductions" (70, p. xxii).

Fifth, both structuralist and systems theories reveal
certain similarities in their historical development. [12] Just
as systems theory was originally conceived as a counter-
actant to the mechanistic or atomistic approach of the physical sciences and "piecemeal investigations, " structuralism
emerged in mathematics as an opposition to compartmen-
talization, "which it counteracts by recovering unity through
isomorphisms. " Similarly, in other fields such as linguistics, psychology, and biology, structuralism is "chiefly
a departure from ... isolated ... phenomena [e.g., linguistics, etc.] ... has long combatted the atomistic ten-
dency to reduce wholes to their prior elements [e.g.,
psychology]" (67, p. 4). [13]

The comparison of Piaget's structuralist theory with
general systems theory may be carried further: first, by
stating the basic concepts of structuralism (as recast by
Piaget), and second, by identifying the underlying conceptual
issues incorporated in structuralism. Piaget's "notion of

structure is comprised of three key ideas: the idea of
wholeness, the idea of transformation, and the idea of self-
regulation." The notion of wholeness thus is a basic concept in both structuralist and systems theory; wholeness is
distinguished from aggregates or composites of elements.

> To insist on this distinction is not to deny that
> structures have elements, but the elements of a
> structure are subordinated to laws, and it is in
> terms of these laws that the structure qua whole
> or system is defined. Moreover, the laws govern-
> ing a structure's composition are not reducible
> ... they confer on the whole as such overall
> properties distinct from the properties of its ele-
> ments [67, pp. 5, 7]. [14]

Consideration is given to both the nature and the mode of
formation (versus preformation) of wholes--and these considerations are relevant to all areas of science. Piaget's
perspective avoids "atomism" and also holism (emergent
totalities). Instead, he offers operational structuralism
which

> ... adopts ... a relational perspective, according
> to which it is neither the elements nor a whole
> that comes about in a manner one knows not how,
> but the relations among elements that count ...
> the logical procedures or natural processes by
> which the whole is formed [67, pp. 8-9].

The subject of part-whole relations is basic to both
systems and structuralist theories. Spiegel's transactional
theory also deals with this. He states that the transactional
field has a pattern, a structure in which all parts are interdependent; in other words, the investigator is looking for
"a pattern which will relate parts to whole." However,
Spiegel also comments on the fact that "It is not that the
whole is greater then the sum of its parts. Rather, the

whole is a way of exhibiting the functional relation between
parts. Whole and parts are complementary and indispens-
able to each other" (87, p. 41). Piaget depicts part-whole
relation from a somewhat different perspective.

> Since the elements in a field are always subordi-
> nated to the whole, every local modification en-
> gendering a refashioning of the ensemble, the first
> law of perceptual totalities is that the whole over
> and beyond its having qualitative features of its
> own, has a quantitative value different from that
> of the sum of its parts. That is to say, the laws
> of composition for perceptual wholes is non-addi-
> tive [67, p. 56].

The question of formation of structures has received
much attention in the systems and discipline sciences.[15]
Piaget's position supporting the idea of the genesis of structures, therefore, has significance--both theoretically and
empirically. He believes that structures are not "static
forms" in that (in addition to their property of wholeness)
they are also systems of transformations. It is not enough
to view structures as wholes, because the laws of structured
wholes are, by their very nature, structuring. "It is a
constant duality, or bipolarity, of always being simultaneously structuring and structured"; in other words, a structure's laws of composition govern the transformations of
the system which they structure (67, p. 10). While all
known structures are systems of transformation, transformation may be either a temporal or non-temporal process.
Piaget emphasizes the explanatory import of the idea of
transformation and the relation between transformation and
formation. One of his central themes (in all varieties of
structures) is the relation between structuralism and constructivism.

Self-regulation, the third basic property of structures, suggests the system notions of steady state and stability. Whereas the idea of structures as transformation systems conveys Piaget's concept of reciprocal assimilation, the idea of structures as self-regulating systems conveys Piaget's notion of accommodation and conservation. "These properties of conservation along with stability of boundaries despite the construction of indefinitely many new elements presuppose that structures are self-regulating" (67, p. 14). As noted above, Piaget explains self-regulation partly in terms of cybernetics; for example, transformational systems that "unfold in time" are governed by feedback regulations (the interplay of anticipation and correction). Self-regulation is also explained in terms of simpler structural mechanisms, "such as pervade biology and human life at every level ... self-regulation ... of a much more elementary sort." Thus, the self-regulating and self-maintaining mechanisms of structures viewed developmentally (as stages) consist of rhythm, regulation, operation (67, pp. 15-16).

Piaget's point that self-regulation may be achieved by various procedures or processes and can be ranked in order of complexity reflects the same theoretical approach of the information-processing control systems model explicated by both Peterfreund and Bowlby with respect to the sequential development of behavioral systems--simple to complex. Although their terminology differs somewhat, both Bowlby and Piaget (within a biological and evolutionary orientation) cite recent studies of ethologists with respect to "a complex structure of instincts" (67, pp. 50-51). Whereas Bowlby explicates the sequential development of behavioral systems mediating instinctive behavior, Piaget states that it is possible

> ... to speak of a 'logic of instincts' whose several
> 'levels' can be subjected to analysis, the hierarchy
> of instincts thereby becoming a 'logic' of organs
> or organic instruments antedating the logic of acts
> (organic activities that are not 'genetically pro-
> grammed') or of manufactured instruments. But
> what is no less essential is that contemporary
> ethology tends to show that all learning and re-
> membering depend upon antecedent structures....
> Thus, the contacts with experience and the fortu-
> itous modifications due to the environment on which
> empiricism modeled all learning do not become
> stabilized until and unless assimilated to structures;
> these structures need not be innate, nor are they
> necessarily immutable, but they must be more
> settled and coherent than the mere gropings with
> which empirical knowledge begins [67, p. 51].

Thus, Piaget emphasizes the formational (versus preforma-
tional) nature of instincts and the way the complex structure
of hierarchy of instincts is incorporated within the modern
view of the evolutionary process. [16]

Although Piaget credits Bertalanffy with introducing an
explicitly structuralist perspective into biology, he suggests
that recent scientific developments "tell us more about the
contemporary structuralist orientation of biology" (67, pp.
46-47). Despite this statement, his conceptual orientation
to self-regulation appears somewhat similar to Bertalanffy's.
First, Piaget states that initial self-regulation is due to
simpler structural mechanisms (e.g., rhythm and general
self-regulation), while Bertalanffy emphasizes that primary
regulation of the organism results from dynamic interaction
within a unitary system and that structured (feedback) arrangements are developed subsequently (see p. 15, Ch. 1).
Second, Piaget like Bertalanffy, believes that organic self-
regulation (animate systems) goes beyond physical

mechanisms of equilibration (inanimate systems), just as organic, unlike physical, structures take account of "meanings" (67, pp. 47-48).[17] Perhaps the crucial difference in their views (Piaget's and Bertalanffy's) hinges on the much-debated use of the term <u>homeostasis</u>, which Bertalanffy employs in the "narrow" sense and Piaget in the "broad" sense. While Piaget comments upon Waddington's introduction of the term <u>homeorhesis</u>[18] with regard to embryology, he explains that the concept of homeostasis is not limited to physiology. Just as Waddington's embryological research led to a theory of "genetic assimilation," ethological studies have demonstrated "genetic homeostasis" (i.e., the fixation of acquired characteristics). Thus, whereas Bertalanffy, Rapoport and other systems theorists generalize the organismic notion to the notion of organized system, Piaget generalizes the notion of self-regulation (of structural systems), which "should be carried beyond the individual organism, beyond even the population, to encompass the complex of milieu, phenotype, and genetic pool" (67, pp. 48-50).

These considerations of notions of self-regulation and homeostasis, in the context of structuralist and information-processing systems theories, reflect many variations in interpretations: in part as terminological or semantic differences; in part as "real" differences regarding the nature of the relationships in man, nature and society; and in part as current "voguish" biases. For example, Bertalanffy, in accord with the humanistic approach to systems theory--and like humanistically-oriented social psychiatrists (e.g., Gray) and psychologists (e.g., Allport)--goes "beyond the homeostasis model"[19] and emphasizes the proactive, creative, stimulus-seeking behavior of living organisms,

especially man (16, p. 40). [20] On the other hand, Bowlby
and Peterfreund, as well as Piaget, accept the concept of
homeostasis; within their biological-evolutionary orientation,
homeostasis is viewed as basic to man's adaptation and
survival.   Whereas Piaget employs the term homeostasis
in connection with self-regulating structures applicable to
all "system levels" and varieties of structures--from biological to societal--Bowlby and Peterfreund employ the concept of homeostasis within the information-processing control
system model.

In explicating his "Point of View" (Chap. 1), Bowlby
cites "a behavioural form of homeostasis" as one of the
central concepts--in addition to those of control, information,
negative feedback.   He also distinguishes between the concept
of homeostasis and the Freudian principle of inertia.   The
latter has been subject to many interpretations; Bowlby,
however, conceives the inertia principle

> ... as a tendency for the level of excitation to
> be reduced to zero while homeostasis is conceived
> not only as a tendency for levels to be maintained
> between certain positive limits but as working to
> limits set mainly by genetic factors and at points
> that maximise the likelihood of survival [18, p.
> 18].

In other words, the Freudian principle of inertia derives
from physics, whereas homeostasis derives from biology
and is compatible with the principle of constancy. [21]

Peterfreund, also writing about homeostasis in the
context of complex control systems, specifically makes the
connection between homeostasis and stress;[22] he refers to
both the subjective psychological aspects and to the physiological aspects of stress, suggesting that "the goal of
reducing stress and maintaining homeostatic conditions is

a basic goal which guides the learning organism in its
choice among various possibilities" (65, p. 200). In other
words, homeostasis and stress are significant notions in
understanding learning and decision-making processes, i. e.,
allowing the input of new information which, when processed,
permits distinctions between "good" or "bad" choices.
Finally, this brief commentary on the concept of homeostasis
and its various interpretations[23] suggests that currently
there are basic (not simply terminological) theoretical differences with respect to the nature and "limits" of man's
adaptability and models of man and environment.

This chapter on the "changing faces of theory" has
focused upon three specific works devoted to theory-revision
in the context of modern scientific knowledge. Analysis of
these theoretical approaches led to comparisons between
the systems theory-model and the structuralist theory-model
as conceived and applied by Bowlby and Peterfreund (systems
model) and Piaget (structuralist model). Certain significant
similarities and commonalities were identified: notions of
wholeness and self-regulation, homeostasis or steady state,
feedback mechanisms (in the development of information-
processing control systems and in the development of self-
regulating transformational structures), levels in hierarchical
arrangements, [24] structure, function, and history, and change
processes. [25] Additional similarities between systems and
structuralist theories included: their biological and evolutionary framework; their emphasis upon interdisciplinary,
cyclic, and converging developments in modern scientific
theory; their historical and parallel theoretical developments
in diverse fields--and related conceptual issues, such as
the controversy between vitalistic or teleological and

mechanistic or reductionistic theories and its resolution in modern twentieth-century science (e. g., information theory, cybernetic theory, and so forth).

Chapter 5

THEORY AND MODEL BUILDING

INTRODUCTION

This examination of "changing faces of theory" requires that particular consideration be given to key conceptual revisions and modifications identified in Bowlby's
instinct theory, Peterfreund's psychoanalytic theory, and
Piaget's structuralist theory. However, it is also recognized that both theoretical and practice developments are
inseparable from problems of terminology and semantics. [26]
These theory revisions, thus, will "reactivate" familiar
issues and will involve further analysis of distinctions between the language of scientific schemes and explanatory
concepts and the language of persons (as vehicles of communication) and subjective expressions of feelings and
emotions. Thus, problems of terminology and semantics
may be understood in relation to: one, the generation of
theory, including its stage of development, its relationship
to other relevant theories, and so forth; two, the distinction between the language of science and theory and the
language of persons (the latter is frequently referred to as
the language of feeling or "clinical" language); three, the
distinction between terminology (and its usage) and "meaning" related to various factors, such as the theoretical
orientation, the situational or "communicational" context;
four, the variation in usage and the relative value of

redefinition and/or standardization of terminology versus
the value of discarding outmoded terminology and substi-
tuting new terminology in the process of theory change and
development. These considerations have particular import
for theory-revisions that explicitly deal with "outmoded"
models, with departures from traditional viewpoints, with
new conceptual tools (explanatory and predictive) that call
for new language. [27] This brief commentary regarding
terminology and semantics introduces the two final parts of
this section: first, the identification and comparison of
theory-revisions presented by Peterfreund, Bowlby and
Piaget; second, the re-view of several basic conceptual
notions and issues as they are clarified, modified and integrated within the information-processing systems model
of Peterfreund and Bowlby and the structuralist model of
Piaget.

CONCEPTUAL REVISIONS AND UPDATINGS

The theoretical revisions of Peterfreund and Bowlby,
as noted earlier, are strikingly similar. This is not surprising since both authors explicitly utilize an information-
processing systems model in updating psychoanalytic and
instinct theory; both clearly designate which traditional
conceptual notions are discarded and why, which are re-
tained and for what purpose, which "alternate" models and
positions are employed and how these are "put to work" in
the psychoanalytic process (Peterfreund) and in the organization of behavioral systems mediating instinctive behavior
(Bowlby). Both Peterfreund and Bowlby place primary
emphasis upon their rejection of the notion of psychic energy
and the "psychical energy model"; that is, they reject the

"economic" and "dynamic" viewpoints of psychoanalytic
metapsychology--these include, in addition to psychic energy,
notions of drives (discharge of drive, neutralization of drive,
etc.), primary and secondary processes, and the pleasure
principle. Psychic energy is derived from the physics and
chemistry of the second part of the 19th century and is,
therefore, an outmoded unscientific notion which separates
psychoanalysis from modern scientific theory. In other
words, psychic energy (sexual and aggressive) is not com-
parable or connected to physical energy. The psychical
energy model "is a model of motivation that assumes the
existence of a special form of energy" (distinct from physical energy). Moreover, as Bowlby states,

> Freud's instinct theory, the pleasure principle,
> and the traditional theory of defence are three
> examples out of many that could be cited of formu-
> lations which, because they are cast in terms of
> a psychical model are ... unsatisfactory as they
> stand [18, p. 20].

According to Peterfreund, the notion of psychic energy
implies a "hydrodynamic" model of man; that is, psychic
energies are assumed to have forces and properties of fluids
which can be transferred. These "innumerable imponder-
able fluids" are organized, integrated, and controlled by
the "ego." In this way, Peterfreund joins the concept of
psychic energy to the concept of ego, both of which are
"characteristic of early scientific thought, of viewing nature
anthropocentrically, as existing only for and in relation to
man, and of using its effects on man for principles of explanations." Thus psychoanalytic theory (using the notions
of psychic energy and ego) "has found it necessary to postulate a typically 19th-century vitalistic anthropomorphic

concept (ego) to explain the nature of control, adaptation, regulation, integration, and organization (65, pp. 54-57). [28] While Bowlby does not explicitly reject the notion of ego as a vitalistic, anthropmorphic concept, as does Peterfreund, he does not utilize the concept of ego in his "alternative model of instinctive behavior." For example, he describes psychological development in human beings as

> characterised not only by simple systems' being
> superseded by goal-corrected systems, but also
> by the individual's becoming increasingly aware of
> the set-goals he has adopted, by his developing
> increasingly sophisticated plans for achieving them,
> and by his increasing ability to relate one plan
> to another, to detect incompatibility between plans
> and to order them in terms of priority. In psy-
> choanalytic terminology these changes are described
> as being due to the supersession of id by ego [18,
> pp. 153-154].

In essence, then, both Peterfreund and Bowlby discard the notions of psychic energy, the pleasure principle, primary and secondary processes, and the notion of the psychic structure as these are conceived in traditional psychoanalytic theory; and they both substitute the systems model for its explanatory concepts--e. g. , information-processing, feed-back.

The notions of conscious and unconscious, unlike the notion of psychic energy, are not rejected by either Peter-freund or Bowlby. On the contrary, both recognize the "clinical" value of these notions and their import for the psychoanalytic process. However, Peterfreund and Bowlby recast conscious and unconscious processes in information-processing terms; for example, both authors discuss conscious and unconscious processes in the context of the appraisal and selecting processes within the information-

systems model; "awareness" and "being felt" express the
notion of the "conscious," but have greater explanatory significance. In other words, notions of conscious and unconscious are valid clinical empirical generalizations rather
than explanatory theoretical concepts. The distinction is a
significant one, stated and reiterated by Peterfreund and incorporated in Bowlby's expositions of appraisal and selecting
processes and problems of terminology.

     Peterfreund "sets the stage" for considerations of
terminological confusions. He explains the nature of scientific theory, the hierarchical levels of scientific explanation,
and distinguishes between empirical generalizations and theoretical laws. He stresses this idea "because the complexity
of the phenomena dealt with in neurology, psychology, and
psychoanalysis has resulted in much serious confusion--
among other things, in the persistence of primitive anthropomorphizations" (65, p. 33). The language of persons is
used to represent psychological experiences and it is the
language of clinical psychoanalysis; the language of persons
is very different than the conceptual language appropriate to
the nervous system. Confusion arises, however, when the
words of persons or feelings are applied to organic or
physiological systems. Stated differently, the various levels
of explanation require different appropriate languages. In
his analysis of the notions of psychic energy and ego,
Peterfreund emphasizes that they do not involve scientific
principles of explanation but represent metaphorical descriptions characteristic of the language of personal experiences.
It is important thus to recognize that clinical language often
employs anthropomorphizations for the purpose of communication; these may be viewed as metaphors or primitive

theories. [29]   Finally, Peterfreund cites the concepts of conscious and unconscious processes as illustrations of the confusion of languages in current psychoanalytic theory.

> Current psychoanalytic theory generally attributes
> many aspects of conscious experience to an un-
> conscious system, e.g., fantasies, wishes, affects.
> It is as if the theory postulated an unconscious
> consciousness. To some extent this problem
> arises from the fact that it is useful and meaning-
> ful at the clinical level to think of unconscious
> fantasies, thoughts and feelings. But at a theo-
> retical level, to avoid a confusion of languages,
> another approach must be taken [65, p. 65].

In his discussion of notions of affect, feeling, and emotion (as part of the appraisal and selecting processes in information-control systems), Bowlby notes that "feeling, attention, and consciousness go together.... Thus, whether or not appraisal processes are felt is probably of considerable consequence for the behavior that emerges." In other words, feeling may be a phase in the appraising processes; if so, "modification of standards of appraisal and of models of environment and organism ... and changes in future behavior" are possible. Bowlby discusses the confusion that often arises in verbalizations or "explanations" of feelings and emotions. Like Peterfreund, he concedes "the tremendous convenience of the vernacular language of feeling" but also comments upon its "dangers."

> Instead of being regarded as indices of how situa-
> tions are being appraised and what behaviours are
> being activated, feelings are reified.... When the
> language of feeling becomes an obstacle to recog-
> nising that feeling entails action of particular
> sorts, it is best abandoned and replaced tempor-
> arily by a language of behaviour [18, pp. 119-
> 123]. [30]

Piaget, as might be expected, does not include a discussion of psychic energy or psychic structure (id. ego, and superego in psychoanalytic theory) in his exposition of structuralist theory. He does, however, refer to conscious and unconscious processes in connection with the nature of psychological structures, distinctions between the individual subject and the epistemic subject, the nature of cognitive life and the degrees of complexity of thought. Essentially, Piaget distinguishes between the subject's consciousness and his achievements or the <u>outcome</u> of his intellectual activity; he distinguishes between consciousness and behavior: "psychological structures do not belong to consciousness but to behavior (only when there is some sort of dis-adaptation does the individual become aware of structures, and this awareness is always quite dim and partial)" (67, p. 99). Stated differently, Piaget emphasizes that cognitive structures (and their construction) belong to the subject's operational behavior and not to his consciousness. Nevertheless, he does not negate the individual subject as a "superfluous entity" since it is the individual subject that is the "center of functional activity." This is consonant with his thesis that cognitive structures are not static and that "structures are inseparable from performance, from functions in the biological sense of the word" (67, pp. 68-70).

Whereas the construction of cognitive structures does not belong to the subject's consciousness, "the whole of cognitive life is linked to structures which are just as unconscious as the Freudian Id, but which reconnect knowledge with life in general" (67, p. 131). Piaget points out that, "psychogenetic studies have shown [that] the mechanisms on

which the individual subject's acts of intelligence depend
are not in any way contained by his consciousness, yet
they cannot be explained except in terms of 'structures'"
(67, p. 138). In many ways, thus, Piaget's approach to
conscious and unconscious processes is similar to that of
Peterfreund and Bowlby, who do not negate notions of conscious and unconscious processes but recast them as different aspects of information-processing. They, too, distinguish between subjective aspects of consciousness and
behavior; between feeling and action and the relationship
between them--i. e., input and processing of sensory data
leading to output which is monitored and regulated (goal-
corrected).

Piaget relates the notion of consciousness to the
levels or degrees of complexity of thought;[31] in the genesis
of thought or cognition, the subject's activity moves from
"spontaneous intellectual egocentricity" toward

> ... a continual 'de-centering' ... which is the
> true 'generator' of structures as constantly under
> construction and reconstruction. The subject
> exists because, to put it very briefly, the being
> of structures consists in their coming to be, that
> is, their being 'under construction' [67, pp. 139-
> 140].

The problem of genesis viewed as transition from one structure to another is, in fact (if not in terminology), very much
like the development of behavioral systems and the organization of behavior conceptualized in the control systems model
(e. g., from fixed action patterns to goal-corrected behavior;
from chain-linked to plan-hierarchy organizations of behavior).[32] In sum, Peterfreund, Bowlby, and Piaget, in
their discussions of conscious and unconscious processes,

do not negate or reject these notions but recast them in
their theoretical models (information-control systems model
and structuralist model). This is significant in clarifying
the much-debated definition of "personality." In their view
(Peterfreund's, Bowlby's, and Piaget's), personality is not
an isolated entity nor is it merely a reflection of social
interaction; instead, personality is viewed as an ongoing,
evolving correspondence, matching, or patterning between
the individual and his environment.

RE-VIEW: THREE BASIC CONCEPTS IN INFORMATION-CONTROL SYSTEMS AND STRUCTURALIST MODELS

The final part of this section will present a brief review of several basic conceptual notions that have appeared
in the entire book and are crucial aspects of the issues and
themes delineated. The concepts of structure, function, and
adaptation may be differentiated and interrelated within a
particular theoretical model. The discussion here will focus
upon these concepts as they are presented and integrated
within the information-processing control systems model (as
employed by Peterfreund and Bowlby) and the structuralist
model (as employed by Piaget). Despite differences in theoretical schemes and terminology, [33] there is an impressive
convergence in the ways in which the three authors explicate
these concepts and the implications they have for a fuller
understanding and deeper appreciation of man and his environment. The first "key" to their convergences and
commonalities is the evolutionary biological frame of reference that underpins their conceptual models and theoretical
revisions. The second "key" is their incorporation of modern scientific concepts within their theoretical models, and

the use of these concepts to update psychoanalytic, instinct, and structuralist theories.

Structure

Both Peterfreund and Bowlby, as well as Piaget, explicate the basic concepts of their respective theoretical models: for example, Peterfreund and Bowlby explicate the concepts of control systems involving notions of information-processing, feedback, and so forth, as they are applied to the development of hierarchically arranged behavioral systems; Piaget explicates the basic notions of structures, as for example, wholeness, transformation and self-regulation. In other words, Piaget starts out with the notion of structure and develops this further as he proceeds from mathematical and logical structures (groups), physical and biological structures, psychological structures, linguistic structures, and structures in the social sciences (sociological, economic, anthropological). Thus, he examines structures as they appear in different fields, or, in systems terms, at different system levels.

Piaget's analysis of structures is the basis of his theoretical exposition and is broader in scope than the analyses given by Peterfreund and Bowlby, who concentrate primarily on the development and hierarchy of human behavioral systems. Nevertheless, the three authors reveal similarities in their definition of and orientation to "structure," and also all three give consideration to certain similar issues: for example, the relationship between structure and function, distinctions between biological and psychological structures, the genesis of structures, the hierarchical arrangement of structures, and the relationship between

structures and causality. Whereas Peterfreund and Bowlby
discuss the concepts of structure and function in the context
of information-processing feedback regulated systems, Piaget
interweaves information and feedback concepts in explicating
the nature and development of structures. For example,
Piaget states that the organism is "the paradigm structure"
and that it gives us "the key to a general theory of structure"; that physical structures are independent of us but
"correspond to our operational structures"; that action as
the source of operations leads to "general coordinations
[that] involve certain elementary structures sufficient to
serve as point of departure for ... more complex construc-
tions" (67, pp. 43-44). And later, when discussing psychological structures, Piaget refers to "some 'copy' of reality
... [or structures] as coordinations of all instruments of
representation" (67, p. 72).

These few references suggest similarities between
Piaget's conceptualization of structure and those of Peterfreund and Bowlby. According to Peterfreund, "The concepts of structure, process, function, and history are basic
biological concepts ... they are different views of information-processing control systems." Both Peterfreund and
Bowlby, like Piaget, conceive of structures as hierarchically
arranged, developing from simple to complex and integrating
phylogenetic and ontogenetic biological history (65, pp. 141-
142). In other words, Peterfreund, Bowlby, and Piaget
emphasize the ongoing evolving nature of structures as well
as their genesis or their past. They concur that the past
is a part of the existing structure and they also concur in
distinguishing between biological and psychological structures.
Whereas Piaget writes about the individual versus the

epistemic subject in his clarification of the nature of cognitive structures (versus experiential psychological phenomena), Peterfreund points out that

> ... one of the very serious difficulties of current
> psychoanalytic theory is that the concept of struc-
> ture is defined in psychological terms ... inas-
> much as psychological experiences are phenomena
> or manifestations resulting from the activity of
> biological structure, it is only the biological struc-
> ture that can change or develop--the underlying
> material entities where information from the past
> is stored. Psychological phenomena per se have
> no history; they are transient manifestations of
> the activity of structures that exist at the moment;
> they parallel or correspond to processes: changes
> over time of matter, energy, and information [65,
> pp. 141-143]. [34]

Bowlby also elaborates upon the biological and physiological
aspects of structure.

> In the case of biological systems, structure takes
> a form that is determined by the kind of environ-
> ment in which the system has in fact been oper-
> ating during its evolution, an environment that is
> of course usually, though not necessarily, much
> the same as that in which it may be expected to
> operate in the future [18, p. 47].

He explains that structures, in the different types of behavioral systems (simple to complex), involve information
that is stored, processed, and retrieved within the central
nervous system and the brain. In fact, it is these (biological) structures that are the source of the individual's
"working" environmental and organismic models necessary
for survival and adaptation (18, pp. 80-82). [35]

Function

        The concept of function is given many definitions,
depending upon its significance and usage in a particular

field or discipline. Bowlby and Peterfreund accept and employ the concept of function as it has been defined by systems theorists. In fact, Peterfreund quotes J. Miller's explication of the terms structure, function, and process; he views function as one form of process--namely, regular recurrent changes or reversible actions. Process, including function, reflects "the organism and its information-processing systems longitudinally, over a period of time" (65, p. 141).[36] The frames of reference, as well as the particular theories with which these authors are concerned, highlight the concept of function as a basic biological process "taking an evolutionary position in which the human mind is viewed as a manifestation of the activity of one of a series of evolving organic forms" (65, pp. 100-101). While Bowlby also uses the concept of function within a biological orientation and systems model, he focuses on the functions of behavioral systems and other consequences of their activity. "In biology that consequence which a system appears as though designed to achieve is usually termed the system's function.... Functions are the special consequences that arise from the way a system is constructed" (18, pp. 125-126). Moreover, Bowlby distinguishes function from causation and also from the notion of predictable outcome.

Most systems theorists (and also Piaget) emphasize the interactional nature of causation, the primacy of "efficient versus final causes," and the relative nature of final ends or outcomes. Bowlby, however, concretizes these notions in his detailed expositions of animal and human behaviors. For example, he negates the teleological idea that the future determines the present through some type of "finalistic causation." Thus, "causes are the factors that lead the system to become active or inactive on any one occasion ... and [the function of a system] has nothing to do with the immediate causes of activity." Function, then, depends upon a system's construction, and in biological systems, "the function of the system is that consequence of the system's activity which led to its having been evolved, and which leads to its continuing to remain in the equipment of the species" (18, pp. 126, 127).

This is not to say that an active biological system has only functional consequences; put differently, not all of the consequences of the activity of a behavioral system are functional; indeed, many may be adverse. Bowlby makes the important point that in the individual, instinctive behavior is absolutely independent of function, whereas in a population of individuals functions must be fulfilled (for at least some of the time by some individuals). It may be recalled that Piaget also employs this notion in his emphasis upon the distinction between the individual subject and the epistemic subject. Essentially then, the predictable outcome is a property of a particular behavioral system in a particular individual, whereas function is a property of that behavioral system in a population of individuals. It is clear that the information-processing control system model as applied by Peterfreund and Bowlby, and the structuralist model as applied by Piaget, view the individual in terms of his biology and in terms of the evolution of his species.[37]

Piaget similarly uses the term function within a biological frame of reference. He takes an "affirmative" stand with regard to the value of the concept of function. He stresses the connection between structure and function-- "structures are inseparable from performance, from func-

tions in the biological sense of the word" (67, p. 69). In
his view (cognitive) structures are self-regulated and self-
maintained because of their functional activity. Function
(used as a biological term) is responsible for the formation
of structures; in cognitive development for example,

> ... assimilation is the functional aspect of struc-
> ture-formation, intervening in each particular case
> of constructive activity, but sooner or later lead-
> ing to the mutual assimilation of structures to one
> another, and so establishing ever more intimate
> inter-structural connections [67, pp. 71-72].

In his discussions of structuralism in the social sciences, Piaget reiterates his affirmation of the concept of
function. For example, he re-emphasizes the constructivism
of structuralism (in contrast to the notion of "static" structures). He also gives attention to Parsons' "structural-
functional" method, pointing out Parsons' connection between
structure and function and Parsons' way of linking functions
to values. Rules (or norms) generated by structures can
change their function, and value points up the dimension of
function: "thus, the duality and re-established interdependence
of value and norm seem to testify to the necessity of distinguishing and connecting structure and function" (67, p.
103). [38] In analyzing anthropological structuralism, Piaget
cites and takes issue with the "anti-functionalist" position of
Levi-Strauss. He points out that it is necessary

> to coordinate sociological and anthropological struc-
> turalism with biological and psychological struc-
> turalism.... And one thing is clear, in biology
> and psychology structural analysis must, at all
> levels, from homeostasis to operations, be sup-
> plemented by functional considerations [67, p.
> 109]. [39]

Finally, Piaget notes that it is the functional aspects of social

structures which account for "a rapprochement between
'formation' and 'response,' as in Waddington's theories."
In this way "a structure changes its function to meet new
social needs" (67, p. 118).   And in his concluding chapter,
there is reemphasis on the import of function in structuralist theory.   "The concept of function has obviously lost
none of its value; all talk about self-regulation involves the
idea of function" (67, p. 142).

Adaptation

The concept of adaptation may well be considered
the conceptual pivot of this chapter.   All theory-models and
practice applications of the human professions require a
concept of adaptation that incorporates humanistic values
with modern scientific knowledge of man and his environment.   Essentially, a "model of adaptation" is based upon
conceptual constructs of the individual-system, the environ-
ment-system, and the ways in which they are interrelated. [40]
The writer's viewpoint is that adaptation is a relational
notion and a notion of order relations.   Stated differently,
adaptation incorporates and interrelates concepts of structure,
function, and history, just as it incorporates and interrelates concepts of the individual-system and the environment-
system; it is a manifestation of the interactive nature of
causality and processes of change and stability.   In essence
then, adaptation involves a patterning, a correspondence, a
matching, or a "fitting," within and between structures or
systems; as such, adaptation is a form of order relations
which is always relative rather than absolute.

The theoretical models employed by Peterfreund,
Bowlby and Piaget (information-control systems and structuralist models) postulate and explicate adaptation as a

biological and evolutionary construct. All three authors
utilize information-processing and feedback regulation as
the key scientific explanatory concepts underpinning the notion
of adaptation. The important point here, however, is that
adaptation is not a property of individuals but a property of
populations and the result of biological and evolutionary development. The teleonomic[41] characteristics of organisms
are adaptations which develop in the course of evolution;
they are associated with the reduction of stress, the maintenance of homeostasis and biological order. As Peterfreund states, "learning, adaptation, and biological order
are, in a sense, synonymous" (65, p. 189). Adaptation,
thus, is depicted by Peterfreund, Bowlby and Piaget as a
biological and evolutionary concept, as a relative issue,
and as a manifestation of correspondences and patternings
(via information-feedback mechanisms, assimilation processes,
and so forth) that result in an inseparable relationship between life and thought, system and environment.[42] Put
differently, ongoing order and change are mirrored in the
integral relationship of the organism and the external
environment.

Additional conceptual and terminological notions are
suggested in the writings of Bowlby and Piaget. The former
notes that "the concept of adaptation in biology is a dif-
ficult one"--because of this he gives particular attention to
and explicates in detail the concept of "adaptation: system
and environment." Bowlby discusses the "equipment" of the
organism that makes possible its adaptation to the environment (or at least to the particular part of that environment
with which it is concerned). Fundamentally, it arises out
of the organism's capacity to perceive patterns. "In all

such cases, we must suppose, the individual organism has
a copy of that pattern in its CNS and is structured to react
in special kinds of ways when it perceives no such pattern."
It is because man is able to perceive certain parts of the
environment (as a pattern) and to use that knowledge to
develop a map of the environment that he is able (with
effector equipment) to achieve his set-goals (18, pp. 47-50).
In order to clarify the notion of adaptation and the relationship between system and environment, Bowlby distinguishes
between and defines concepts of adaptation and adaptedness.
He recognizes the "limits" of adaptation in his emphasis
upon the fact that no system can be so flexible that it suits
all and every environment; thus it is necessary to consider
simultaneously the structure of a system and also the environment within which it is to operate.

> The system's environment of adaptedness ... in
> the case of a biological system ... is the environ-
> ment within which the system gradually became
> evolved. Because of this distinction it is some-
> times useful to refer to the environment of adapted-
> ness of a man-made system [inanimate] as its
> environment of designed adaptedness and to that
> of a living organism as its environment of evolu-
> tionary adaptedness [18, p. 50].

Since concepts of adaptation and adaptedness pose
terminological or semantic difficulty, Bowlby distinguishes
between the condition of being adapted, that is, a state of
adaptedness, and the process of becoming adapted. A state
of adaptedness is ascribed to the structure of the organism,
and the property of being adapted entails reference both to
a specified outcome and to a specified environment. The
process of becoming adapted, on the other hand, refers to
a change of structure: one, a change whereby the structure
continues to attain the same outcome but in a different

environment; two, a change whereby the structure attains
a different outcome in the same or a similar environment.   The term adaptation is often employed to denote the
process of change that leads a structure to become adapted
(either to a new environment or to a new outcome), but it
may also be employed to denote the condition of being adapted.
In order to avoid this confusion Bowlby terms the condition
of being adapted as "adaptedness."   The latter terms are
incorporated in Bowlby's theoretical model of instinctive behavior and the development of behavioral systems; thus, the
term "environment of adaptedness" is a basic conceptual
notion in Bowlby's exposition.   Since adaptedness is relative
and since adaptation may involve not only the organism's
change of structure (to attain the same or different outcome)
but also a change in environment, Bowlby poses the further
distinction between the terms adapt and adaptation (as applied
to change of structure of the organism), and the terms
modify and modification (as applied to environmental change).
In other words, Bowlby reserves the terms adapt and adaptation for changes occurring in the organism-system, and the
terms modify and modification for any change of the environment that facilitates the more effective operation of the
organism-system. [43]

In his explication of terminological problems related
to the concept of adaptation, Bowlby (like Peterfreund and
Piaget) emphasizes that adaptedness is a property of a
population and not of an individual.

> The biological unit, or system, to which the con-
> cept 'adapted' applies, is not, therefore, an in-
> dividual but an interbreeding population.   This
> population is made up of individuals that together
> carry a unique collection of genes, known as the
> population's gene pool, and inhabits a particular

environment of evolutionary adaptedness, known as
its ecological niche [18, p. 56].

His elaboration of "man's environment of adaptedness" includes a commentary on Hartmann's concept of "man's
ordinary expectable environment." Unlike Rabkin, he accepts,
in a general way, Hartmann's notion, but believes that his
own term (man's environment of evolutionary adaptedness)

> ... is defined more rigorously in terms of evo-
> lution theory. Not only does ... [it] make even
> more explicit that organisms are adapted to par-
> ticular environments but it draws attention to the
> fact that not a single feature of a species' mor-
> phology, physiology, or behaviour can be under-
> stood or even discussed intelligently except in
> relation to that species' environment of evolution-
> ary adaptedness [18, p. 64].

In other words, he believes that his terminology makes more
comprehensible the "vagaries" of human behavior.

Bowlby's distinctions in terminology with regard to
the concept of adaptation are suggestive of similar distinctions given by Piaget with regard to the concept of equilibrium. When the latter raises the question--how do forms
acquire structural organization?--he provides the answer as
"a general formative process in nature, leading from forms
to structures and establishing the self-regulation constitutive
of the latter." Piaget then points up the significance of the
concept of equilibration in physics, biology, psychology and
in the social sciences. It is

> ... equilibration which accounts for the 'selection'
> of the actual system from among the range of pos-
> sibles; it is equilibration, again, which establishes
> homeostasis at its various organic levels and which
> explains the development of intelligence as well....
> Indeed, once it is recalled that every form of
> equilibrium is definable in terms of a 'group' of

'virtual' transformations and that a state of equilibrium must always be distinguished from the process of equilibration, the processes whereby equilibrium becomes established in these increasingly
complex systems account not only for the regulations characteristic of each level but even for the
form which these regulations take at the final
stage, when they become 'reversible operations.'
The equilibration of the 'cognitive' and the 'practical' functions contains all that is necessary for an
explanation of the rational schemata: a system of
lawful transformations and an opening to the possible,   that is, the two conditions for transition
from temporal formation to non-temporal intercon-
nection [67, p. 113-114].

In sum, Piaget's explication of the concept of equilibration
and his distinction between the state of equilibrium and the
process of equilibration may be viewed as analagous to Bowlby's
explication of the concept of adaptation and the distinction
between adaptation and the state of adaptedness (as well as
his distinction between adaptation applicable to the organism-
system and modification as applicable to the external environment).   Finally, there appears to be a "correspondence"
between Piaget's concept of equilibration and Bowlby's concept
of adaptation in that both concepts refer to the process and
state of the interconnections between the system and environ-
ment--from simple to complex levels of organization.

NOTES FOR PART III

1.   See the earlier sections of the book (Part I and Part
       II) for discussion of general systems theory trends
       and applications.

2.   The role of terminology and semantics was explicated
       at selected points in Parts I and II.   This subject
       is highlighted and further developed in Part III.

3.   Bowlby explains his preference for the term "instinct

theory" as contrasted to the terms "drive theory"
or "motivation theory." Peterfreund, on the other
hand, uses the term "drive theory" although he discusses it in very much the same way as Bowlby
discusses instinct theory, both authors revising
notions of instinct and drive by replacing them in
an information-systems model.

4. This writer recognized the similarities between Bowlby's
    book on attachment and Peterfreund's monograph
    on psychoanalytic theory and, in part, this was the
    initial impetus for writing this section of the book.
    Peterfreund comments in a footnote, "Since comple-
    tion of this monograph, Volume I of <u>Attachment</u>
    <u>and Loss</u> by John Bowlby has been published ... in
    this work Bowlby adopts a theoretical frame of
    reference that is strikingly consistent with the one
    presented here" (65, p. 149).

5. The nature and process of structure formation is a
    dominant concern in Piaget's work; he writes about
    a wide range of structures and his analysis is
    often at a highly abstract level. Bowlby, in the
    context of his analysis of behavioral systems,
    discusses in great detail the notions of structure
    and function (as, of course, does Piaget) and
    questions specifically "how does 'structure' come
    about?" Peterfreund explicates concepts of struc-
    ture, process, function, and history within an
    information-system frame of reference, noting
    that, in accord with the hierarchical arrangement
    of systems, "one can detect hierarchies in struc-
    ture and in process." It is of particular interest,
    however, that much like Piaget, he views phylo-
    genetic and ontogenetic history as an integral part
    of existing structures.... "One of the very seri-
    ous difficulties of current psychoanalytic theory is
    that the concept of structure is defined in psycho-
    logical terms" (65, pp. 141, 142, 143). Finally,
    Peterfreund introduces structure formation in
    relation to the problem of learning; although "learn-
    ing refers to many different processes," his ap-
    proach is an informational one in which "learning
    takes place at different times and in different
    circumstances, and various existing structures
    may evolve differently" (65, p. 205).

6. Whereas Bowlby, in his discussion of ontogeny, con-
   ceptualizes the development of behavioral systems
   and the ways in which primitive behavioral systems
   are elaborated and then superseded by sophisticated
   systems, Piaget refers to this developmental process as a change from behavior organized on the
   basis of sensori-motor intelligence to behavior
   organized on the basis of symbolic and precon-
   ceptual thought.

7. Baldwin, in Theories of Child Development, writes
   that,

   > Piaget transfers two features of biological evolu-
   > tion to his theories of the development of the
   > individual. One is the continuous fitting of old
   > structures into new functions, and the develop-
   > ment of new structures to fill old functions under
   > changed circumstances. Development is solidly
   > rooted in what already exists and displays a
   > continuity with the past. At the same time, the
   > structure changes to fit new demands. Second,
   > these adaptations do not develop in isolation.
   > All of them form a coherent pattern so that the
   > totality of biological life is adapted to its en-
   > vironment [65, pp. 365-366].

   This quotation illustrates the evolutionary and biological approach characteristic of Piaget, Peterfreund, and Bowlby; it presents the core of developmental theory and incorporates notions of structure
   and function, change and adaptation, notions which
   are at the center of systems and discipline sciences.

8. Peterfreund's "translation" of Piaget's concepts into
   information systems terms does not coincide with
   Piaget's conceptualization of these concepts within
   the structuralist frame of reference. In his most
   recent publication, Structuralism, Piaget states,

   > ... all such behavior that has innate roots but
   > becomes differentiated through functioning con-
   > tains, we find, the same functional factors and
   > structural elements. The functional factors are
   > assimilation, the process whereby an action is
   > actively reproduced and comes to incorporate
   > new objects into itself ..., and accommodation,

the process whereby the schemes of assimilation
themselves become modified in being applied
to a diversity of objects. The structural elements are, essentially, certain order relations
..., subordination schemes ... and correspondences.... As the primary assimilation schemes
become mutually coordinated ('reciprocally
assimilated'), certain equilibriated structures,
those that make for a modicum of 'reversibility,'
become established [67, p. 63].

9.   Peterfreund explains that Piaget is interested in the
      ways in which man organizes the world vis-a-vis
      inanimate objects, whereas psychoanalysis is in-
      terested in the ways the world is organized pri-
      marily vis-a-vis animate objects; he also makes
      the point that the latter is "a general state of
      affairs often subject to pathology in contrast to the
      former which is less subject to pathology" (65,
      p. 377).

10.   The reader is undoubtedly aware of the fact that Piaget's
      Structuralism was not available to either Peter-
      freund or Bowlby prior to or during the period in
      which they completed their respective publications
      on psychoanalytic theory and instinct theory.

11.   Piaget's "conclusion" quoted here is very similar to
      Bertalanffy's statement regarding parallel develop-
      ments to systems theory. After identifying the
      features that these theories have in common, he
      states that,

            An important consideration is that the various
            approaches enumerated are not, and should not
            be considered to be monopolistic. One of the
            important aspects of the modern changes in
            scientific thought is that there is no unique and
            all-embracing 'world system' [12, p. 14].

12.   Of particular import is Gray's reference to Piaget's
      studies on language and learning as one of the or-
      ganismic theories contributing to the development
      of general systems theory and also his discussion
      of Gestalt psychology as one of the parallel develop-
      ments to general systems theory (31, pp. 11, 22-

23). Piaget's analysis of Gestalt psychology, however, differs from Gray's.

13. Piaget discusses sequentially mathematical and logical
structures, physical and biological structures,
psychological structures, linguistic structuralism,
structural analysis in the social sciences, and
finally, structuralism and philosophy. In regard
to the latter, Piaget observes that currently "we
find structuralism tackling historicism, functional-
ism, sometimes even all theories that have recourse to the human subject" (67, p. 4).

14. Piaget utilizes the term "emergent" in a somewhat
different sense than systems theorists. According
to the latter, wholes have emergent properties
which derive from the relations between the elements and from the whole (as contrasted to its
elements in isolation). According to Piaget, however, emergence and the theory of emergence
simply reverses the position of the atomist; the
whole thus is viewed as the result of some law of
nature, not subject to further analysis. Indeed,
Piaget rejects the notion of emergence (as he
employs the term) in all areas of sciences--
physical and biological structures, psychological
structures and social structures; whereas Gestalt
psychologists correctly:

remind us that a whole is not the same as a
simple juxtaposition of previously available
elements ... [but] by viewing the whole as
prior to its elements or contemporaneous with
their 'contact,' they simplified the problem to
such an extent as to ... [by-pass all] questions
about the nature of a whole's laws of composition.

Subsequently, Piaget points out that

... to note the existence of wholes at different
levels and to remark that at a given moment the
higher 'emerges' from the lower is to locate a
problem, not to solve it ... Durkheim's structuralism, for example, is merely global, because he treats totality as a primary concept

explanatory as such; the social whole arises
of itself from the union of components; it
'emerges' [67, pp. 8, 46, 98].

15. See the discussion of this issue in earlier sections
     devoted to trends in general systems theory and
     applications in social work and psychiatry.   It
     may be recalled, for example, that Rabkin rejects
     the idea of performism which he considers to be
     inherent in psychoanalytic theory and in the concep-
     tion of epigenesis as employed by Erikson, Hart-
     mann, and others.   Rabkin also specifically rejects
     the notion of social structure, not because of its
     "global" nature but because it is subject to the
     dangers of the "organismic analogy" and reduction-
     ism.   Rabkin, like others, substitutes the ecological
     model, and notions of transaction, network, inter-
     face, for the concept of social structure (giving his
     own definition of these terms).   It was noted
     earlier that many social workers, as well as social
     psychiatrists, currently reject structure as a static
     concept and also reject the notion of genesis (in
     accord with the ecological and transactional view-
     points).

16. It is of particular interest that both Piaget, a psycholo-
     gist writing from his structuralist perspective, and
     Rabkin, a social psychiatrist, cite Waddington's
     embryological studies which clarify the notion of
     epigenesis.   Piaget discusses the concept of epi-
     genesis as redefined by Waddington, because it
     negates the idea of preformation, reestablishes
     "the role of the environment as setting 'problems'
     to which genotypical variations are a response,"
     all of which contribute to modern evolutionary
     theory.   Rabkin, as noted earlier, rejects the
     notion of epigenesis as used in psychoanalytic
     theory and ego psychology, because it conveys
     "preformism."   Thus Rabkin also redefines epi-
     genesis, not in terms of structuralism, but in
     terms of the ecological approach and the network-
     interface model.   Peterfreund, discussing learning
     and structure formation in "the full sweep of evo-
     lutionary processes--phylogenetic Darwinian processes
     and ontogenetic learning," refers to the recent
     work of Waddington in clarifying certain aspects
     of phylogenetic Darwinian theory.   He also

comments upon the import of stress factors in
phylogenetic Darwinian processes. Like Piaget,
he indicates that Waddington clarified the complex
feedback relationship between organism and environment: "it is clear that the organism is not simply
passive in relation to the selecting environment; to
some extent the organism chooses the very environment that exerts the selective pressure on it" (65,
p. 213). Thus, while Rabkin utilizes the re-defini-
tion of epigenesis to support his ecological viewpoint, Peterfreund utilizes the re-defined notion
of epigenesis to explicate and support his information-processing systems model, both phylogenetically
and ontogenetically. Although Bowlby, like Peterfreund, uses the information-processing control
systems model and updates instinct theory in light
of modern scientific knowledge, he does not refer
specifically to the notion of epigenesis nor to Waddington's research.

17. Earlier in the book it was noted that although Bertalanffy
believes in the continuity of nature, he emphasizes
distinctions between animate (living) versus inanimate (non-living) theoretical models.

18. Homeorhesis refers to "a kinetic equilibration in embryological development whereby deviations from
certain necessary paths of development are
compensated for" (67, p. 49).

19. It may be recalled that most systems theorists (e.g.,
see Miller) consider the notion of dynamic steady
state as one of the key concepts of systems. The
term steady state is distinguished from the term
homeostasis by some theorists in order to avoid
the purely biological meaning in which homeostasis
is conceived as a fixed equilibrium rather than a
steady state or balance that is in dynamic flux.
Some systems theorists, as indicated above, employ the term homeostasis in a broader sense because its generalization is valid; some systems
theorists also use the term homeostasis--for
example, when discussing family systems--recog-
nizing that the term is then used metaphorically
(e.g., see 47, p. 430). Finally, other systems
theorists have broadened the term homeostasis

to heterostasis, which accounts for change as well as balance and suggests the "circular motion in all human activity" (31, pp. 23, 48).

20. Systems theorists, psychiatrists, and psychologists who emphasize the creative, proactive nature of man might appear to share a common orientation. However, analysis of the stances of these theoreticians and practitioners reveals some important differences. Bertalanffy, like other systems theorists, does not concur with many (currently popular) "growth" personality theories primarily concerned with notions of "self-realization," "self-actualization," and so forth. The latter terms have little value in the context of systems theory; Bertalanffy suggests that system goal-seeking and goal-setting (based on information-processing and feedback concepts) are more useful as well as valid constructs.

21. It would appear that Bowlby's control system model incorporates notions of homeostasis and system constancy; this is compatible with Piaget's principle of conservation within his structuralist theory.

22. In light of the discussion of crisis theory in the preceding section of the book, it is of interest to note that Bowlby, Peterfreund, and Piaget make no reference to crisis theory as such--within either the information-processing systems model or the stucturalist model. Bowlby, however, does include considerations of "sensitive" or "critical" periods in the development of behavioral systems.

23. The concept of homeostasis was discussed earlier in the context of general systems theory, parallel theories, and other theoretical approaches utilized by social work and psychiatry (see Parts I and II). It may be noted here that Spiegel's transactional theory emphasizes the import of homeostatic mechanisms in the role system. "The chief homeostatic or regulative mechanism in the [social] system is the complementarity of roles ... the equilibrium state of the system is directly proportional to the degree of complementarity in the roles" (87, pp. 117, 316-317).

24. Bowlby and Peterfreund explicate the hierarchical

arrangement of behavioral systems in the context
of information-processing control systems theory;
Piaget explicates the genesis of intelligence and
the sequential phases of intellectual development in
the context of "levels" of psychological structures
(67, pp. 62-68). Hierarchical levels of structures
(whether organic or social) are based on transformation processes; thus a structure may be

> ... considered a substructure of a larger one;
> but in being treated as a substructure, a struc-
> ture does not lose its own boundary; the larger
> structure does not 'annex' the substructures; if
> anything, we have a confederation, so that the
> laws of the substructure are not altered but
> conserved and the intervening change is an en-
> richment rather than an impoverishment [67,
> p. 14].

25. The principle of equifinality is basic to open system and
general systems theory. (See earlier sections,
Part I and Part II.) Although Bowlby and Peterfreund explicate the basic constructs and principles
of information-processing and systems theory in
updating instinct and psychoanalytic theories, they
do not explicitly refer to equifinality; however, it
is implicit in their discussions of development and
change processes. Piaget also does not refer to
the notion of equifinality as such. Nevertheless,
he cites three basic principles involved in self-
regulation (characteristic of all structures), one
of which is that "the end result is independent of
the route taken" (67, p. 20).

26. A number of such problems have been considered in
the foregoing discussions. For example, the
definition and use of the term homeostasis, the
definition and meaning of the term emergent (and
emergence), the definition and redefinition of the
term epigenesis, the definition of the concept of
structure (as applied to physical, biological, psychological, and social system levels), and of course,
theoretical and terminological debates with respect
to the concept of systems, concepts of the individual, the environment and their interrelation-
ship, and so forth.

27. The issue of concepts and semantics may be illustrated
    in models other than systems and structuralist
    theories. Spiegel's discussion of a theory of col-
    lective violence includes a pertinent commentary
    on the notion of stress.

    > During the Age of Anxiety ... psychosomatic
    > and psychiatric research was based on the con-
    > cept of 'stress,' an internally experienced cor-
    > relate of anxiety ... both psychological and
    > social research have shifted, in some degree,
    > to more externally defined problems of be-
    > havior ... this transformation does highlight
    > the need for new definitions and concepts [87,
    > pp. 340-341].

28. Peterfreund's discussion of psychic energy as a "hy-
    drodynamic" notion involving imponderable fluids
    is very similar to Rabkin's analysis. That is,
    Rabkin, like Peterfreund, rejects the notion of
    psychic energy as based upon "chemical-physical
    forces inherent in matter" (69, p. 113). There
    is also concurrence in that both view psychic
    energy as a teleological formulation. Neverthe-
    less, their analysis of other "inner-space" con-
    cepts differs in a number of respects, including
    their choice of a theoretical model to substitute
    for traditional psychoanalytic metapsychology.

29. Peterfreund quotes Nash in his commentary on the
    anthropomorphizations of psychoanalytic theory
    (65, p. 72). The dangers of analogical and
    metaphorical thinking have been referred to in the
    earlier discussion of general systems theory, and
    it is an important consideration in the analysis of
    psychoanalytic, instinct and structuralist theories.
    Although metaphoric thinking is typically regarded
    as primitive or unscientific, it does, however,
    serve several scientific functions, a number of
    which have been implied in the above discussion.
    For example, metaphor may be useful for com-
    munication purposes, for serving as the "germ" of
    an unfolding idea, thus generating theory, and the
    analysis of metaphor often leads to a better
    appreciation of theory. Nash states that "a
    jumbled theory rooted in metaphor can sometimes

be put in order by laying bare and disentangling its figurative roots. " He also indicates that complexity of metaphor can be confusing--"but tangled thinking occurs in the absence of metaphor, as in its presence. " It is of interest that he cites the sharp criticism directed toward the psychoanalytic concept of the unconscious: "the notion of the unconscious is the most prolific metaphor that has yet arisen in psychology. " Finally, Nash refers to Masserman's conclusions on this subject:

> One scarcely doubts that most metaphors encountered in scientific discourse have little importance for science. That some metaphors play a useful role in the generation and analysis of scientific theory does, however, refute the idea that metaphor is intrinsically unscientific, and figurative thinking beyond the bounds of scientific concern. The value of any individual metaphor is, of course, an empirical matter, which can only be decided by considering the benefits conferred by the metaphor in question, and the difficulties it entails [61, pp. 337, 340-342].

The import of language and semantics is also basic to Piaget's analysis of structuralism in diverse fields. Writing about the development of thought and the nature of the human mind, Piaget (referring to the works of Levi-Strauss) observes that the "metaphor ... constituting a 'first' or 'primary' form of discursive thought ... must it not mean that there is something to follow after, or at least that there are 'levels'?" (67, p. 115).

30. Peterfreund's and Bowlby's discussions of feelings, emotions, affects, and also notions of conscious and unconscious processes are quite different from Rabkin's analysis and rejection of all "innerspace" concepts, not simply the notion of psychic energy. It may be recalled that Rabkin considers concepts of affect, the unconscious, and so forth, as totally invalid, having no utility for psychoanalysis or social psychiatry. Although Rabkin gives "lip service" to the compatibility of theories of individual and social psychiatry, in essence he

rejects all psychoanalytic concepts and in so doing
he puts "inner-space" concepts into "outer-space."
    Spiegel's presentation of transactional theory
does not include a critique of psychoanalytic "inner-
space" notions. Moreover, he employs psychoanalytic concepts and terminology in his family
analyses, e.g., the ego and ego mechanisms, the
conscious and unconscious. In his discussion regarding problems of terminology, however, Spiegel
explicates thought and action as different but related aspects of behavior. "Thought but not action
tends to float away from behavior." This is due
to the dimension of time and its function and also
to the nature of thoughts and actions as systems
of behavior. Thoughts are more easily systema-
tized than actions and "a system of thought or a
system of belief ... presents itself as more dis-
crete than a system of action ... [which is] more
extended in space-time ... [and] more fluid" (87,
pp. 11-13).

31.   In his presentation of "the beginnings of structuralism
in psychology," Piaget refers to the experimental
work of K. Buhler; the latter showed that there
are ascending degrees of complexity in thought,
and differentiated three stages. The first is consciousness, "thought as independent of images and
as ascribing significance"; the second is "consciousness of the rules involved in relational structures"; the third is "the deliberate synthetic act
'intent upon' the construction of a whole, that is,
a system of thought 'at work'" (67, p. 53).

32.   Both Bowlby and Peterfreund discuss the development
of behavioral systems and their hierarchical arrangements at considerable length. Bowlby gives
a great deal of attention to the ways in which
behavioral systems develop and also the ways in
which they are coordinated and organized.

33.   Their (Peterfreund's, Bowlby's, and Piaget's) different
emphases and different contexts enrich and enhance the meanings of these concepts and their
interrelationships.

34.   In discussing the nature of learning in the context of
phylogenetic evolutionary processes, Peterfreund

reiterates his rejection of structures as "something psychological or experiential" instead of reserving the term <u>structure</u> for "material entities where information can be stored" (65, p. 157).

35. Bowlby, as indicated above, discusses the relationship between information-processing and the development of environmental and organismic models. He notes the importance of conscious mental processes in building models, revising, extending, checking their consistency, or utilizing them in developing "a novel plan to reach a set-goal.... Unless a model is subjected from time to time" to becoming conscious, it is unlikely that behavior patterns can be scrutinized and changed (18, pp. 82-83).

36. See the earlier sections (Parts I and II) for definition and discussion of these concepts. It should be noted that Spiegel uses general systems theorists' definitions of structure and function. For example, he states that they are both aspects of process; structure appears as the static aspect, whereas function is the dynamic aspect of the same basic process. In the context of his transactional theory, he observes that "formal structures of concrete systems arise through transactional processes within and between systems ... transactionally considered, structures are merely aspects of systems." Spiegel also explicates the relationship between structure and function, e.g., a structure exhibits a function, and brings their relationship "into concordance" using both transactional and systems terminology. His particular focus, however, is on the relationship between structure and function in the social role system (87, pp. 28, 113-115).

37. In his chapter on Function, Bowlby makes the interesting point that the function of "long-recognised" behavioral systems have not yet been fully determined. In a later chapter focused on "attachment behavior" of the young child, Bowlby argues that this is an example of instinctive behavior and he advances a hypothesis regarding the function of this attachment behavior.
     Bowlby considers "problems of terminology" in the concluding part of his chapter on Function.

He explains, for example, why he does not employ
the noun "instinct" but does employ the adjective
"instinctive"; he also discusses such terms as
"need," "wish," "aim," and "purpose." The reasons given for rejecting the terms instinct, need,
wish, aim, and purpose and the reasons for his
employment of the terms instinctive and set-goal
are explicated in the context of his theoretical
model.

38. Piaget also gives attention to the problem of structure
     and function in the field of economics. In this
     context he stresses "this primacy of functioning
     which distinguishes economic structures." Eco-
     nomic structures are characterized by the primacy
     of activity, and economic equilibration or self-
     regulation is of the feedback type (67, p. 104).

39. Piaget discusses Lewin's field theory in his analysis of
     psychological structures. He raises serious
     questions about Lewin's "field of force" and also
     his field hypothesis "with its various anti-function-
     alist consequences" (67, p. 57). As noted earlier
     (Chap. 3), Spiegel does not employ the Lewinian
     notion of field in his transactional theory; he re-
     fers to Maxwell for his orientation to field as the
     subject of investigation. Moreover, Spiegel, like
     Piaget, utilizes the concept of function in his
     transactional approach and he distinguishes and
     connects structure and function as well as value
     and norm in social role systems. For example,
     he writes of the function of social norms in
     establishing standards of patterning social roles
     and the import of value orientation as a trans-
     formational concept. "The transition from norms
     governing social roles to the meanings given those
     role activities within the culture occurs through the
     rank-ordering of value orientations" (87, pp. 52-
     53). Finally, it may be pointed out that while
     many systems theorists (e.g., Buckley) have
     challenged Parsonian social system theory because
     of its "conserving orientation" which does not take
     account of the processes of change in complex
     systems, both Piaget and Spiegel cite Parsons'
     structural-functional model as a valuable contri-
     bution.

40.   It may be recalled that Rabkin explicates the basis for
      his rejection of the adaptive model formulated by
      ego psychologists (e.g., Hartmann). He takes
      issue with Hartmann's notion of an "average
      expectable environment" and he states that

           ... like the germ theory the adaptive model
           is reductionist in that it simplifies complex
           issues, and it also blocks relevant paths of
           inquiry. The adaptive model masks environ-
           mental differences, just as the social psychi-
           atric model tends to mask individual differences;
           both models would be more effective if confined
           to their specific areas of competence and rele-
           vance [69, pp. 134-141].

41.   The term teleonomic is the modern biological concept
      of "the apparently purposive nature of organisms"
      (Peterfreund quoting Simpson, 65, p. 113).

42.   Most systems theorists and theorists employing systems
      concepts incorporate and frequently explicate no-
      tions such as "matching," "fitting," "patterning."
      Some of the authors quoted in this book--e.g.,
      Gordon, Bowlby, Piaget, Spiegel, and others--
      emphasize the import of notions of "fit" and "pat-
      tern" in system-environment relationship. See
      also the writings of Geoffrey Vickers on disor-
      ganization of behavior and adaptability (93, 94).

43.   In Spiegel's transactional viewpoint, adaptation or ad-
      justment is characterized by "mutually regulative
      processes" mediated by the exchange of communi-
      cation in the relationship between two people.

           Organizational adaptations ... [distinguished
           from 'organizational defenses'] ... are secon-
           dary processes called forth within the group
           organization of the family to settle the role con-
           flicts which have given rise to a symptomatic
           episode or crisis ... they appear more fre-
           quently in 'well' families than in 'sick' families.
           They are characterized by the use of internal
           or external agents who perform as buffers for
           the dis-equilibrium, as go-betweens or referees,
           or as models for the solution of the conflict
           [87, pp. 314, 307].

PART IV

CONCLUDING STATEMENT

The trends, themes, and issues identified and discussed in this book have been emphasized and documented in different ways and in different contexts. A summary therefore, seems unwarranted; only a brief concluding statement follows.

The question may well be raised, why is this theory analysis needed and what is its justification? Obviously, it was with "conscious awareness" that this book was focused upon theory and presented at a theoretical level; that is, it is theoretical in its scope and content. There is, of course, the hope that profits will accrue from a theoretical approach. Kurt Lewin has often been quoted as saying: "There is nothing so practical as a good theory." It must be admitted, however, that the writer's specific interest here was to provide a more comprehensive approach to an understanding of significant theories relevant to social work and to other human professions. The theoretician and/or practitioner might thereby obtain a wider perspective of his own and others' theoretical conceptions and biases. Currently we hear and read much about the breadth of social work's knowledge base, its broader conceptual orientation to social services, its increasingly wider range and diversity of

practice roles and techniques. Nevertheless, there is the
possibility that: one, this breadth is illusory and, two,
it is the result of borrowing numerous "faddist" notions
which are encompassed within or combined with many traditional notions--often without a full appraisal or appreciation
of their meanings and their correspondences.

This book, thus, is a response to a number of such
current beliefs and practices. First, in taking the long
view of general systems theory and other theories we may
be enabled to obtain a grasp of the origins of relevant
theories and their flow. Second, in explicating conceptual
and terminological issues (and debates) we may enhance our
knowledge and determine what positions we wish to assume
and why. Third, in offering a comparative analysis of three
selected theoretical revisions it may be possible to extend
our horizons, to recognize that there are similar and different theoretical orientations and conceptual models with
which we are as yet unfamiliar but which may offer untold
opportunities to advance the state (and status) of social work.
In other words, the last section of this book was conceived
as both a conclusion and an introduction. Social work cannot afford at this time to limit itself to currently popular
theoretical and practice "vogues"; it cannot afford to remain
provincial and isolated in its scientific-professional frame
of reference. Finally, to quote Piaget,

> Only by withdrawing somewhat from the immediate
> present ... [will we be able] to appraise what is
> currently being said.... Only by a continual 'de-
> centering' ... [which will make us] enter upon,
> not so much an already available and therefore ex-
> ternal universality, as an uninterrupted process of
> coordinating and setting in reciprocal relations
> [67, pp. 137, 139].

REFERENCES

1. Allport, F. H, "Self-Regulation and Self-Direction in Psychological Systems, " in F. H. Allport, Theories of Perception and the Concept of Structure. New York: Wiley, 1955.

2. Allport, Gordon W., "The Open System in Personality Theory, " in Walter Buckley, Modern Systems Research for the Behavioral Scientist. Chicago: Aldine Publishing Co., 1968.

3. _____, Pattern and Growth in Personality. New York: Holt, Rinehart and Winston, Inc., 1961.

4. Arieti, Silvano, "Toward a Unifying Theory of Cognition, " in W. Gray et al. (eds.), General Systems Theory and Psychiatry. Boston: Little, Brown & Co., 1969.

5. Ashby, W. Ross, "General Systems Theory as a New Discipline, " General Systems, 3:1, 1958.

6. Auerswald, Edgar, "Interdisciplinary versus Ecological Approach, " in W. Gray, et al. (eds.), General Systems Theory and Psychiatry. Boston: Little, Brown & Co., 1969, pp. 373-386 (Family Process, 7:202-215, 1968).

7. Bell, Norman W., and Ezra P. Vogel (eds.), A Modern Introduction to the Family (rev. ed.). New York: The Free Press, 1968.

8. Bellak, Leopold, and Leonard Small, Emergency Psychotherapy and Brief Psychotherapy. New York: Grune & Stratton, 1965.

9. Bertalanffy, Ludwig von, "General System Theory and Psychiatry, " in S. Arieti ed.), American Handbook of Psychiatry, Vol. 3. New York: Basic Books, 1964.

10.   , "An Outline of General System Theory,"
British Journal of the Philosophy of Science, Vol. 1,
1950.

11.   , "General System Theory," General Systems
Yearbook, Vol. 1, No. 4, 1956.

12.   , "General System Theory: A Critical Review,"
General Systems Yearbook, Vol. 7, 1962 (also in
W. Buckley, 1968).

13.   , Problems of Life. New York: Wiley, 1952.

14.   , "The Mind-Body, A New View," Psychosomatic Med., 26:29-45, 1964.

15.   , Robots, Man and Minds. New York:
Braziller Co., 1967.

16.   , "General Systems Theory and Psychiatry--
An Overview," in W. Gray, et al. (eds.), General
Systems Theory and Psychiatry. Boston: Little,
Brown & Co., 1969, pp. 33-51.

17. Boulding, Kenneth E., "General Systems Theory: The
Skeleton of Science," Management Science, Vol. 2,
No. 3, April 1956 (also in Buckley, 1968).

18. Bowlby, John, Attachment (Vol. I). New York: Basic
Books, 1969.

19. Buckley, Walter, Sociology and Modern Systems Theory.
New York: Prentice-Hall, 1967.

20.   , (ed.), Modern Systems Research for the
Behavioral Scientist. Chicago: Aldine Publishing
Co., 1968.

21. Caplan, Gerald, An Approach to Community Mental
Health. New York: Grune & Stratton, 1961.

22. Carlson, Virginia, et al., "Social Work and General
Systems Theory," Group Research Project Under
the Faculty Supervision of Gordon Hearn, University of California, Berkeley, School of Social Wel-
fare, 1957.

23. Carroll, Edward J., "Steady State and Change in Family

Interviews," in W. Gray, et al. (eds.), General Systems Theory and Psychiatry. Boston: Little, Brown & Co., 1969.

24. Chin, Robert, "The Utility of Systems Models and Developmental Models for Practitioners," in Warren G. Bennis, et al. (eds.), The Planning of Change: Readings in the Applied Behavioral Sciences. New York: Holt, Rinehart and Winston, Inc., 1961.

25. Coser, Lewis, "The Functions of Conflict," in N. J. Demerath and Richard A. Peterson, System, Change, and Conflict. New York: The Free Press, 1967.

26. Duhl, Frederick, "Intervention, Therapy and Change," in W. Gray, et al. (eds.), General Systems Theory and Psychiatry. Boston: Little, Brown & Co., 1969.

27. Duhl, Leonard, "Planning and Predicting: Or What to Do When You Don't Know the Names of the Variables," in W. Gray, et al. (eds.), General Systems Theory and Psychiatry. Boston: Little, Brown & Co., 1969.

28. Ellis, David O., and Fred J. Ludwig, Systems Philosophy. Englewood Cliffs: Prentice-Hall, 1952.

29. Erikson, Erik, "Identity and the Life Cycle," Psychological Issues, New York: International Universities Press, Inc., Vol. I, No. 1, 1959.

30. Gordon, William E., "Basic Constructs for an Integrative and Generative Conception of Social Work," in Gordon Hearn (ed.), The General Systems Approach: Contributions Toward an Holistic Conception of Social Work. New York: Council on Social Work Education, 1969.

31. Gray, William, et al. (eds.), General Systems Theory and Psychiatry. Boston: Little, Brown & Co., 1969.

32. Grinker, Roy R. (ed.), Toward A Unified Theory of Behavior. New York: Basic Books, Second Edition, 1967.

33. _____, et al., Psychiatric Social Work; A Trans-
    actional Case Book. New York: Basic Books,
    1961.

34. _____, "Symbolism and General Systems Theory,"
    in W. Gray, et al. (eds.), General Systems Theory
    and Psychiatry. Boston: Little, Brown & Co.,
    1969.

35. Gross, Bertram, "The Coming of General Systems
    Models of Social Systems," Human Relations,
    Vol. 20, No. 4, 1967.

36. Haley, Jay, Strategies of Psychotherapy. New York:
    Grune & Stratton, 1963.

37. Hall, A.D., and R.E. Fagen, "Definition of System,"
    in W. Buckley (ed.), Modern Systems Research
    for the Behavioral Scientist. New York: Aldine
    Publishing Co., 1968.

38. Hansell, Norris, "Patient Predicament and Clinical
    Service: A System," in W. Gray, et al. (eds.),
    General Systems Theory and Psychiatry. Boston:
    Little, Brown & Co., 1969.

39. Hearn, Gordon (ed.), The General Systems Approach:
    Contributions Toward an Holistic Conception of
    Social Work. New York: Council on Social Work
    Education, 1969.

40. _____, Theory Building in Social Work. Toronto:
    Toronto University Press, 1958.

41. Hollis, Florence, "And What Shall We Teach," Smith
    College Studies for Social Work, Vol. 42, No. 2,
    June 1968, pp. 184-196.

42. Jackson, Don, "The Individual and the Larger Contexts,"
    in W. Gray, et al. (eds.), General Systems Theory
    and Psychiatry. Boston: Little, Brown & Co.,
    1969, p. 387 (also in Family Process 6:134-147,
    1967).

43. Kahn, Alfred J., (ed.), Shaping the New Social Work.
    New York: Columbia University Press (in
    press).

44. Kaplan, Abraham, The Conduct of Inquiry. San Francisco: Chandler Publishing Co., 1964.

45. Katz, Daniel, and Robert L. Kahn, The Social Psychology of Organizations. New York: John Wiley & Sons, Inc., 1966.

46. Klein, Alan F., "The Application of Social System Theory to Social Work," Paper Presented at Annual Program Meeting of the Council on Social Work Education, New York, January 1966.

47. Laqueur, H. Peter, "General Systems Theory and Multiple Family Therapy," in W. Gray, et al. (eds.), General Systems Theory and Psychiatry. Boston: Little, Brown & Co., 1969.

48. Lathrope, Donald E., "The General Systems Approach in Social Work Practice," in Gordon Hearn (ed.), The General Systems Approach: Contributions Toward an Holistic Conception of Social Work. New York: Council on Social Work Education, 1969.

49. _____, "The Use of Social Science in Social Work Practice: Social Systems," Paper Presented at the National Association of Social Workers' Tenth Anniversary Symposium, Atlantic City, New Jersey, May 1965.

50. Lutz, Werner A., Concepts and Principles Underlying Social Casework Practice. National Association of Social Workers, May 1956.

51. MacIver, John, "Implications of General Systems Theory in Industry and Community," in W. Gray, et al. (eds.), General Systems Theory and Psychiatry. Boston: Little, Brown & Co., 1969.

52. Maruyama, Magoroh, "The Second Cybernetics," General Systems, 8:233, 1963.

53. McBroom, Elizabeth, "Socialization and Casework," in R. Roberts and R. Nee (eds.), Theories of Social Casework. Chicago: Chicago University Press, 1970.

54. Meadows, Paul, "Models, Systems and Sciences,"

American Sociological Review, Vol. 22, No. 1,
February 1957.

55. Menninger, Karl, The Vital Balance. New York: The
Viking Press, 1963.

56. Meyer, Carol H., Social Work Practice: A Response to the
Urban Crisis. New York: The Free Press, 1970.

57. Miller, James G., "Toward a General Theory for the
Behavioral Sciences," American Psychologist, Vol.
10, No. 9, September 1955.

58. _____, "Living Systems: Basic Concepts," Behavioral
Science, Vol. 10, No. 3, July 1965 (reprinted in
W. Gray, 1969, pp. 51-133).

59. _____, "Living Systems: Cross-Level Hypotheses,"
Behavioral Science, Vol. 10, No. 4, October 1965.

60. _____, "Living Systems: Structure and Process,"
Behavioral Science, Vol. 10, No. 4, October 1965.

61. Nash, Harvey, "The Role of Metaphor in Psychological
Theory," Behavioral Science, 8:326-345, 1963.

62. Parad, Howard (ed.), Crisis Intervention. New York:
Family Service Association of America, 1965.

63. Pasewark, Richard, and Dale Albers, "Crisis Intervention: Theory in Search of a Program," Social
Work, Vol. 17, No. 2, March 1972. pp. 70-77.

64. Paul, Norman, "A General Systems Approach to Human
Maturation and Family Therapy," in W. Gray, et al.
(eds.), General Systems Theory and Psychiatry.
Boston: Little, Brown & Co., 1969.

65. Peterfreund, Emanuel, "Information, Systems, and Psychoanalysis," Psychological Issues, Vol. 7, Nos.
1 and 2, New York: International Universities
Press, 1971.

66. Phillips, Lakin E., and Daniel N. Wiener, Short-Term
Psychotherapy and Structured Behavior Change.
New York: McGraw-Hill, 1966.

67. Piaget, Jean, Structuralism. New York: Basic Books,
1968.

68. Polsky, Howard, "System as Patient: Client Needs and System Function," in G. Hearn (ed.), The General Systems Approach: Toward an Holistic Conception of Social Work. New York: Council on Social Work Education, 1969.

69. Rabkin, Richard, Inner and Outer Space. New York: Norton, 1970.

70. Rapoport, Anatol, Foreword in Walter Buckley (ed.), Modern Systems Research for the Behavioral Scientist. Chicago: Aldine Publishing Co., 1968.

71. _____, "The Promise and Pitfalls of Information Theory," Behavioral Science, I (1956), reprinted in W. Buckley (1968), pp. 137-142.

72. Rapoport, Lydia, "The State of Crisis," in Howard J. Parad (ed.), Crisis Intervention. New York: Family Service Association of America, 1965.

73. Rapoport, Rhona, "Normal Crisis, Family Structure and Mental Health," Family Process, March 1963, Vol. 2, No. 1, 1963.

74. Reid, William, and Ann Shyne, Brief and Extended Casework. New York: Columbia University Press, 1969.

75. Rizzo, Nicholas, et al., "A General Systems Approach to Problems in Growth and Development," in W. Gray, et al. (eds.), General Systems Theory and Psychiatry. Boston: Little, Brown & Co., 1969.

76. Rome, Howard P., "Psychiatry and Social Change," in W. Gray, et al. (eds.), General Systems Theory and Psychiatry. Boston: Little, Brown & Co., 1969.

77. Ruesch, Jurgen, "The Old World and the New," American Journal of Psychiatry, 124:225, 1967.

78. _____, "A General Systems Theory Based on Human Communications," in W. Gray, et al. (eds.), General Systems Theory and Psychiatry. Boston: Little, Brown & Co., 1969.

79. Samperi, Florence, "Impressions and Reflections of

Werner Lutz' System Theory for Case Study, Diagnosis and Treatment," Paper Presented in Doctoral Seminar, Columbia University School of Social Work, January 1966.

80. Schefflen, Albert, "Behavioral Programs in Human Communication," in W. Gray, et al. (eds.), General Systems Theory and Psychiatry. Boston: Little, Brown & Co., 1969.

81. Selye, Hans, The Stress of Life. New York: McGraw-Hill, 1956.

82. Shafer, Carl M., "Teaching Social Work Practice in an Integrated Course: A General Systems Approach," in G. Hearn (ed.), The General Systems Approach: Toward an Holistic Conception of Social Work. New York: Council on Social Work Education, 1969.

83. Shulman, Lawrence, "Social Systems Theory in Field Instruction: A Case Example," in G. Hearn (ed.), The General Systems Approach: Toward an Holistic Conception of Social Work. New York: Council on Social Work Education, 1969.

84. Sister Mary Paul Janchill, R.G.S., "Systems Concepts in Casework Theory and Practice," Social Casework, Vol. 15, No. 2, February 1969, pp. 74-82.

85. Sommerhof, G., "Purpose, Adaptation, and 'Directive Correlations'," in Analytical Biology. London: Oxford University Press, 1950 (Chapter II) (also in W. Buckley, 1968, pp. 281-295).

86. Spiegel, John, "Environmental Corrections as a Systems Process," in W. Gray, et al. (eds.), General Systems Theory and Psychiatry. Boston: Little, Brown & Co., 1969.

87. _____, Transactions: The Interplay Between Individual, Family, and Society. New York: Science House, 1971.

88. Stein, Irma L., "The Application of System Theory to Social Work Practice and Education," Paper Presented at the Annual Program Meeting of the Council on Social Work Education, New York, January 1966.

89. _____, "The Systems Model and Social Systems
     Theory: Their Application to Social Work," in H.
     Strean, Social Casework: Theories in Action.
     Metuchen, N. J. : Scarecrow Press, 1971.

90. Stierlin, Helm, "Short Term vs. Long Term Psycho-
     therapy in the Light of a General Theory of Human
     Relationship," British Journal of Med. Psychol.,
     Vol. 41, Great Britain: 1968, pp. 357-367.

91. Strickler, Martin, and Jean Allgeyer, "The Crisis
     Group: A New Application of Crisis Theory,"
     Social Work, Vol. 13, No. 3, July 1967, pp. 28-
     32.

92. Ullman, Montague, "A Unifying Concept Linking Thera-
     peutic and Community Process," in W. Gray, et
     al. (eds.), General Systems Theory and Psychiatry.
     Boston: Little, Brown & Co., 1969.

93. Vickers, Geoffrey, "Is Adaptability Enough?", Behavi-
     oral Science, Vol. 4, No. 3, July 1959.

94. _____, "The Concept of Stress in Relation to the
     Disorganization of Human Behavior," in J. M.
     Tanner (ed.), Stress and Psychiatric Disorder.
     Oxford: Blackwell Scientific Publishing Co., Ltd.
     1959 (also in Buckley (ed.), Modern Systems Re-
     search for the Behavioral Scientist. Chicago:
     Aldine Publishing Co., 1968, p. 354).

95. Watzlawick, Paul, et al., Pragmatics of Human Com-
     munication. New York: W. W. Norton & Co.,
     Inc., 1967.

96. Wiener, Norbert, The Human Use of Human Beings.
     New York: Doubleday Anchor Books, 1954.

97. _____, Cybernetics. New York: Wiley, 1948 (see
     rev. ed. 1961, Cambridge MIT Press).

98. Yinger, J. Milton, Toward a Field Theory of Behavior.
     New York: McGraw-Hill Book Co., 1965.

and inductionism   52-54
and metaphor   137-138(n29)
and organismic analogy   51-52
and (system) hierarchy   49-50, 65
and unification of social work   33-34
      see also   Isomorphism
Anthropology
    and concept of socialization   82(n18)
    and structuralism   92, 94, 117, 122, 132(n12)
      see also   Interdisciplinary approach
Anthropomorphization
    and psychoanalytic concepts   110-11, 112-113, 137-138(n29)
      see also   Analogy; Concepts and terminology;
          Metaphor; Vitalism
Arietti, S.   73
Ashby, W.R.   ix, 9-10, 19
Atomism
    and structuralism   99, 100, 132-133(n14)
      see also   Mechanistic (atomistic) approach; Whole-part
          relations
Attachment (Vol. I)   90, 129
Attachment behavior
    and function as instinctive behavior   140-141(n37)
    and Sensori-motor theory (and control systems model)
        95-96
      see also   Development of behavior; Function; Instinct
          theory
Auerswald, E.   68, 69, 71, 86(n39)

Baldwin, A.L.   130(n7)
Behavior
    and conscious and unconscious processes   113, 114-115
    and ecological and transactional theories   71-72
    and information-communication theory   20-24
    and language   113, 139(n30)
      see also   Personality; Inner space concepts
Behavior modification
    and theory-model   43, 71
      see also   Learning theory; Therapeutic role-strategy
Behaviorism   see   Behavior modification; Ecological theory;
        Learning theory; Transactional theory-model
Bellak, L.   81(n14)
Bertalanffy, L. von   ix, 3, 7, 8, 9, 10, 13-14, 15-16, 17,
        18, 19, 20, 25(n10), 26(n13), 38, 49, 50, 51, 52,
        54, 56, 72, 83(n23), 85(n38), 99, 103, 104, 131
        (n11), 134(n17), 135(n20)
Biological evolutionary theory

156

and structuralist and control systems-model 93-94, 102,
107
and systems theory 18, 24
see also Causality; Self-regulation

Darwin, C. 133-134(n16)
Decision-making
and cybernetics 19-20
and homeostasis and stress 105-106
and information-processing 16-17
see also Information-communication theory; Learning
Development of behavior
and information-processing control systems model 90,
95-97, 102, 111, 115, 117, 124-125, 130(n6), 135(n22),
139(n32), 140(n35)
and structuralist model 102-103, 114-115, 118, 127-128,
130(n7), 130-131(n8)
see also Hierarchy; Organismic-environmental models;
Thought processes
Development of systems
and differentiation and specialization 11-12, 15, 20-21,
22-23, 31, 37, 80(n9), 83(n23)
and de-differentiation 12, 25-26(n11), 83(n23)
see also Entropy-negative entropy; Open system theory;
Pathology (mental illness); System-environment relationship
Deviation amplifying process
and feedback model 21-22
and model applications in social work and psychiatry 37,
81(n12), 84-85(n35)
see also Causality; Cybernetics
Dewey, J. 61
Discipline sciences
and models of structures 26(n18), 99, 103-104, 117-119,
121-122, 132-134(n13,14,15,16), 141(n38)
and models of systems 4, 5, 24(n5), 25(n7), 31-32, 36-
37, 54-55, 78-79(n2,4), 79-80(n7), 80(n10), 141-142
(n39,40,43)
see also Information-processing (control) systems
model; Living-nonliving models; Organismic-environmental models; Structuralism; Translation of theory;
Unification of theory
Dissent ix
Drives
and control systems-model terminology 128-129(n3)
and psychoanalytic theory 109-110
see also Model of physics; Motivation theory

159

Duhl, F.   69, 76, 82(n19)
Duhl, L.   83(n26)
Durkheim, E.   132-133(n14), 133-134(n16)

Ecological theory
    and model of 66-69, 72-73, 84-85(n35), 86(n39, 40),
        133-134(n15, 16)
    and therapeutic approach 71, 75, 82(n19), 85(n36)
        see also Epigenesis (epigenetics); Family therapy;
            Interdisciplinary approach; Interface concept-model;
            Network concept; Personality
Ego
    and crisis theory intervention 40-42
    and ecological and transactional theories 71, 138-139(n40)
    and information control systems and structuralist theories
        110-112, 114
    and social work 39, 64, 80-81(n11)
        see also Concepts and terminology; Inner space con-
            cepts; Psychoanalytic theory
Ego psychology
    and psychiatric theory-models 59, 60, 61, 62, 83(n24),
        133-134(n15, 16), 142(n40)
    and social work theory-models 40, 42, 45, 56-57, 80-
        81(n11), 81(n16)
        see also Crisis theory intervention; Ecological
            theory; Epigenesis (epigenetics); Information-
            processing (control) systems model
Elasser, W. M.   85(n38)
Embryological studies
    and revision of epigenetics 133-134(n16), 134(n18)
    and structuralism 104
        see also Biological evolutionary theory; Ethology;
            Homeorhesis
Emergent
    and concepts and terminology 136(n26)
    and system wholeness 3
    and wholeness of structures 100, 101, 132-133(n14), 136(n26)
        see also Formation and transformation of structures;
            Whole-part relations
Emotions see Affect; Feelings
Energy
    and concept of structure 119
    and entropy 25-26(n11)
    and information-processing 16-17
    and system boundary 25(n6)
    and systems theory and social work 31, 37, 80(n9)
        see also Matter and motion; Psychic energy; System-
            environment relationship

and systems model   19-22, 24, 49
  see also Cybernetics; Information-communication
    theory; Self-regulation
Feelings
  and conscious and unconscious processes   113, 115
  and critique of psychoanalytic theory   138-139(n30)
  and language of   108, 112-113
  see also Affect; Concepts and terminology; Inner
    space concepts
Field theory
  and ecological and transactional models   66-67, 70-71,
    84(n33)
  and structuralism (Lewinian field theory)   84(n34), 141
    (n39)
  see also Hierarchy; Transactional theory
Foci-in-the-field
  and transactional theory   48-49, 53, 62, 68, 71
  see also Concepts and terminology; Field theory
Formation and transformation of structures   95, 100-103,
    121-123, 127-128, 129(n5), 132-134(n14, 16), 135-
    136(n24), 141(n39)
  see also General systems theory; Hierarchy; Prefor-
    mation (preformism); Self-regulation; Structuralism
Function
  and biological evolutionary theory   120-121, 130(n7), 140
    (n37)
  and structuralist theory   121-123, 141(n38)
  and systems theory model   6, 120, 141(n39)
  and transactional theory   140(n36), 141(n39)
  see also Process; Structure; Value
Functions of conflict (The)   26(n16)

General systems theory [GST; Systems theory]
  and model   7-8, 15-16, 52
  and other systems theories   10-24
  and scientific method of study   8-10, 49-54, 98-99
  see also Hierarchy; Information-processing (control)
    systems model; Isomorphism; System-environment
    relationship
General systems theory and psychiatry   85(n37)
Genesis
  and ecological and transactional models   71, 84-85(n35),
    133(n15)
  and social work   57
  and structure (formation)   101, 115, 117, 118
  and system model (history)   6, 8
  and systems and structuralist models   106, 118, 135-136
    (n24)
162

see also Causality; Hierarchy
Gerard, R. W. 25(n7)
Gestalt psychology
    and structuralist theory 26(n18), 132(n14)
    and systems theory 18, 20, 131-132(n12)
        see also Whole-part relations
Gill, M. 62
Goldstein, K. 10
Gordon, W. 34, 78(n1), 80(n8), 80-81(n11), 142(n42)
Gray, W. 18, 20, 85(37), 104, 131-132(n12)
Grinker, R. 6, 7, 8, 48, 58, 63, 70, 71, 73, 84(n30, 31,
        33), 85(n38)
Gross, B. 3
Growth (self-actualization) theories
    and systems theory and psychiatry 60, 135(n20)
        see also Humanism; System goal
GST see General systems theory

Haire, M. 52
Haley, J. 40
Hall, A. D. 7
Hansell, N. 76
Hartmann, H. 127, 133(n15), 142(n40)
Hearn, G. 33, 78(n1)
Heterostasis
    and GST 38, 134-135(n19)
        see also Causality; Concepts and terminology: Homeo-
            stasis; Humanism
Hierarchy
    and levels of scientific explanation 30, 96-97, 111-113,
        137-138(n29)
    and levels of structures 94-95, 102-103, 105, 106, 117,
        118, 135-136(n24)
    and levels of systems 4, 7, 9, 11, 24(n3), 25(n8), 33,
        38, 48-51, 54, 65, 67-68, 69-70, 73-74, 76-77, 82-
        83(n21, 22), 84(n33), 85-86(n38), 129(n5)
        see also Concepts and terminology; Isomorphism;
            Thought processes
Holism see Emergent; General systems theory; Organismic
        theory; Structuralism; Whole-part relations
Hollis, F. 78(n1)
Homeorhesis
    and embryology 104, 134(n18)
        see also Epigenesis; Equilibrium; Structuralism;
            Systems theory
Homeostasis
    and concepts of adaptation and equilibration 124, 127

163

164

Instinct theory
  and behavioral systems 111-112, 120-121, 135(n22), 139
    (n32), 140(n37)
  and biological evolutionary theory 118-127
  and control system model 90, 91-92, 105, 111-113, 118-
    119, 120-121, 124-125
  and Freudian psychoanalytic theory 105, 109-110, 111-112
  and Sensori-motor theory 95-96
  and terminology 113, 125-127, 128-129(n3), 140-141(n37)
    see also Attachment behavior; Conscious and uncon-
      scious processes; Development behavior; Homeostasis;
      Psychic energy
Interdisciplinary approach
  and crisis theory 40, 69-70
  and ecological and transactional models 66, 69, 71-72,
    86(n39)
  and GST and psychiatric theory 58-60, 73-74, 77-78
  and GST and structuralist theory 98-99, 106, 131(n11)
  and GST model 8, 17, 49-54
  and psychoanalytic, instinct, and structuralist theories
    88-89, 90-92, 94-95
Interface concept-model
  and ecological and transactional theories 67-69, 133-134
    (n15, 16)
  and interdisciplinary approach 69, 86(n39)
    see also Communication theory; Network concept
Isomorphism
  and cybernetics 19
  and GST 11
  and GST and psychiatry 65, 67-68, 69, 76, 85(n38)
  and GST and social work 49-50, 54, 57
  and GST and structuralism 89, 99
    see also Analogy; Hierarchy; Homomorphism

Jackson, D. 61, 63, 67, 68, 71, 75, 84(n33), 84-85(n35)
Janchill, Sister Mary Paul 78(n1), 80(n9)

Kahn, A. J. 46
Kamerman, S. 46, 80(n11)
Koestler, A. 83(n22)
Kolakowski, L. ix

Laqueur, H. P. 86(n41)
Laszlo, E. ix
Lathrope, D. 34, 78(n1), 79(n2, 4, 7)

Personality theories see Ego psychology; Growth (self-actu-
     alization) theories; Learning theory; Psychoanalytic
     theory; Social psychiatry
Peterfreund, E. 90-126, 129(n3, 4), 130(n7, 8), 131(n9),
     133-134(n16), 135(n22), 135-136(n24), 137(n28, 29),
     138(n30), 139(n32, 33), 139-140(n34), 142(n41)
Piaget, J. 10, 26(n18), 84(n34), 90, 92-128, 129(n5),
     130(n6, 7), 130-131(n8), 131(n9, 10, 11, 12), 132(n13,
     14), 133-134(n16), 135(n21, 22), 136(n24), 138(n29),
     139(n31, 33), 141(n38, 39), 142(n42)
Pleasure principle
     and information-control systems model 110-111
          see also Psychoanalytic theory
Polsky, H. 34, 78(n1), 79(n4)
Preformation (preformism)
     and concept of structure 101-103, 133(n15)
     and epigenesis 133-134(n15, 16)
          see also Biological evolutionary theory; Ecological
               theory; Embryological studies; Formation and trans-
               formation of structures
Prevention
     and communication theory 47
     and crisis theory intervention 41-42, 44-45, 81(n16)
          see also Community health programs
Primary and secondary processes
     and information-processing control systems model 110,
          111
     and Sensori-motor theory 96-97
          see also Concepts and terminology; Inner space
               concepts; Psychoanalytic theory
Process
     and concepts of structure, function, and adaptation 119,
          120, 122, 125-126, 127-128, 129(n5), 130-131(n8),
          140(n46)
     and psychiatric theories 63-64, 70-71, 75-77, 82(n19),
          84-85(n35), 85(n36)
     and social work theory 34, 37
     and systems theory 5, 6, 16-17, 25(n7), 120
          see also Information-processing (control) systems
               model; Self-regulation
Psychiatric social work: a transactional case book 85(n38)
Psychiatry
     and current theoretical views 60-64, 83(n24, 25)
     and GST 58-60, 73-74, 83(n23)
     and intervention applications 70-71, 74-77, 82(n19),
          83(26), 85(36)
     and social work 64-65, 84(30, 32)
     and variations of systems theories and concepts 65-73,

84(n33), 84-85(n35), 85-86(n38), 86(n39)

Rapoport, R.   40
Reductionism
    and models   54-55
    and organismic analogy   51-52
    and social psychiatry   67-68, 84(n33), 133(n15)
    and system level concept   52-54
        see also   Analogy; Hierarchy; Isomorphism
Release
    and communication theory-intervention   47, 82(n19), 85
        (n36)
        see also   Ecological theory; Therapeutic role-strategy;
            Transactional theory-model
Research
    and cognitive (psychogenetic) studies   92, 95, 96, 97,
        114, 139(n31)
    and crisis theory   40, 81(n13)
    and embryological studies   104, 133-134(n16), 134(n18)
    and ethological studies   102-103
    and GST   9-10
    and instinct and psychoanalytic theory   91-92
    and psychiatry   74-77
    and social work   33-34
        see also   Biological evolutionary theory; Interdisciplinary
            approach
Rizzo, N.   18, 20, 73
Role concepts theory
    and crisis theory   40-42, 45
    and personality theory   52
    and transactional theory   58-59, 62-63, 66, 70, 135(n23),
        140(n36), 141(n39), 142(n43)
        see also   Social system theory; Therapeutic role-
            strategy; Value
Rome, H.   77
Rubenstein, B.   90
Ruesch, J.   58, 63, 73

Schefflen, A.   73
Schemata
    and concept of structure   97
    and equilibration   128
        see also   Sensori-motor theory; Translation of theory
Schwartz, J.   90
Self-regulation
    and structuralist theory and GST   93, 102-106, 122-123,
        127-128, 136(n25), 141(n38)
    and systems theory-model   15-16, 20-21, 26(n17), 31-32,
        38, 56

and transactional theory and GST 140(n36), 141(n39), 142 (n43)
>   see also Adaptation; Equilibrium; Feedback; Homeo-
>   stasis
Selye, H. 26(n15), 40
Sensori-motor theory
>   and control-system model of behavior 95-96, 130(n6, 7)
>   and psychoanalytic theory 96-97, 131(n9)
>   and structuralism 102, 130-131(n8)
>   see also Accommodation and assimilation processes;
>   Aliment, Schemata
Set-goal
>   and information control system model of behavior 43,
>   95-96, 111, 125, 140(n35), 140-141(n37)
>   see also Concepts and terminology; Instinct theory;
>   Sensori-motor theory; System goal
Shafer, C. 78(n1)
Shulman, L. 78(n1)
Simon, H. A. 49, 50
Simpson, G. G. 142(n41)
Social control
>   and social work 32, 48, 79(n4), 82(n18)
>   see also Therapeutic role-strategy
Social planning
>   and GST and psychiatry 74-75, 76-77, 83(26)
>   see also Community health programs; Prevention
Social psychiatry
>   and ecological and transactional models 66-73, 82(n19),
>   83(n26), 142(n43)
>   and GST psychiatric model-applications 73-78
>   and other psychiatric theories 60-64, 138-9(n30), 142(n40)
>   and social work 64-65, 81(n14)
>   see also Crisis theory intervention; Family therapy;
>   Therapeutic role-strategy
Social system theory
>   and ecological model 67, 133(n15)
>   and social work model-applications 33, 79(n4), 82(n18)
>   and structuralism 122-123, 141(n38)
>   and systems constructs 5-6, 25(n7)
>   and transactional theory 135(n23), 141(n39)
>   see also Discipline sciences; Role concepts-theory;
>   Value
Social work
>   and model applications 33-34, 41-42, 44-45, 54-57
>   and other theories 36-41, 84(n30, 32), 86(n39)
>   and psychiatry 39, 64-65, 83(n24)
>   and systems theory-model 29-36
>   see also Crisis theory intervention; Therapeutic

172

and development of   92, 96-97, 115, 130(n6), 138(n29)
    see also   Learning; Sensori-motor theory
Toward a unified theory of behavior   84(n31)
Transactional theory-model
    and concepts of structure, function, and adaptation   140
        (n36), 141(n39), 142(n43)
    and crisis theory   40, 69, 84(n32)
    and homeostasis   135(n23)
    and learning theory   71-72
    and psychiatry   62-63, 66-67, 68, 70-71, 72-73, 84(n31),
        86(n40), 100-101, 141(n39)
    and psychoanalytic theory   139(n30)
    and social work   37, 84(n30), 86(n39)
    and systems theory (GST)   9, 23, 48-49, 51, 53, 55, 72,
        85(n38)
        see also   Field theory; Foci-in-the field; Role concepts-
            theory; Social psychiatry
Transactions: the interplay between individual, family, and
            society   62
Translation of theory
    and information control systems theory and Sensori-motor
        theory   95-97, 130-131(n8)
    and systems theory and crisis theory   45-46, 69-70
    and systems theory and social work   31-33, 38-40, 80-
        81(n11)
        see also   Concepts and terminology

Ullman, M.   73
Unification of theory
    and communication, ecological and crisis theories   68-69
    and GST and psychiatric theory   60-61, 73-74, 83(n25),
        85(n38)
    and GST model   7-8, 49-50, 51-54
    and instinct and psychoanalytic theories and biological
        evolutionary theory   91-92, 94 (Chapters 4 and 5)
    and instinct theory and Sensori-motor theory   95-96
    and systems theory and social work   33-34
    and systems theory and structuralist theory   93-95, 98-
        100
    and systems theory and transactional theory   85-86(n38),
        140(n36)
        see also   Concepts and terminology

Value
    and concept of value orientation 63, 141(n39)
    and concepts of stress and strain   14-15, 26(n16), of

DATE DUE			
OCT 16 '79	OCT 17 '79		
DE 7 '83	DEC 6 '83		
GAYLORD			PRINTED IN U.S.A